THE HORRORS

Charles Demers

THE HORRORS

AN A TO Z OF FUNNY THOUGHTS ON AWFUL THINGS

Douglas & McIntyre

Douglas and McIntyre (2013) Ltd.
P.O. Box 219, Madeira Park, BC, V0N 2H0
www.douglas-mcintyre.com

Cover and interior illustrations by Eduardorama
Edited by Trena White
Cover design by Carleton Wilson
Text design by Carleton Wilson
Printed and bound in Canada on FSC-certified 100% post-consumer fibre

Canada Council for the Arts   **Conseil des Arts du Canada**

BRITISH COLUMBIA
ARTS COUNCIL
An agency of the Province of British Columbia

Canada

Douglas and McIntyre (2013) Ltd. acknowledges the support of the Canada Council for the Arts, which last year invested $157 million to bring the arts to Canadians throughout the country. We also gratefully acknowledge financial support from the Government of Canada through the Canada Book Fund and from the Province of British Columbia through the BC Arts Council and the Book Publishing Tax Credit.

Cataloguing data available from Library and Archives Canada
ISBN 978-1-77162-031-4 (paper)
ISBN 978-1-77162-032-1 (ebook)

For my father, Daniel Demers, whose unshakably
positive outlook on life has been my
only reason for ever questioning his paternity.
Je t'aime fort, fort.

"Tragedy, like its partner comedy, depends on an acknowledgement of the flawed, botched nature of human life—although in tragedy one has to be hauled through hell to arrive at this recognition, so obdurate and tenacious is human self-delusion. Comedy embraces roughness and imperfection from the outset, and has no illusions about pious ideals. Against such grandiose follies, it pits the lowly, persistent, indestructible stuff of everyday life."

—Terry Eagleton

CONTENTS

INTRODUCTION

THAT THERE EXISTS a sometimes infinitesimally short circuit connecting pain to humour is one of the elemental facts of my life, a lesson laid down in the first few minutes of my existence: while the doctor was stitching my mother's torn perineum in the maternity ward, Mom turned to the medic and deadpanned: "Might as well stitch it all the way up, doc—nobody's getting back in there."

My mother's side of the family, the Birnies, have always been good at rattling off one-liners to let you know when they're hurting, even if the jokes come out by accident. When my auntie Laurie was asked, just a few months into her marriage and already frustrated with her husband's overwhelming focus on hockey, "How's married life?" she replied, without intending any wordplay: "It's fine, in between periods." (I was heartbroken when a terrible version of this same joke appeared on the execrable David Spade sitcom *Rules of Engagement*; it was like finding out that Guy Fieri had gotten his hands on an old, beloved family recipe, then battered the results in Cool Ranch Doritos.)

The Birnie family has always moved with ease between tragedy and comedy. My uncle Phil could easily have been a professional comic, and the same was often said about my hilarious mom; people were, I've been told, constantly telling her that she should be on *The Carol Burnett Show*—a compliment she couldn't fully process as one because, inexplicably, she hated *The Carol Burnett Show*. Nevertheless, she was funny enough, *plus* she was redheaded. A lifetime of family get-togethers with cousins and aunts and uncles has run together in my memory as an unending string of jokes, funny anecdotes and recounted pranks, like the time when they were children that my Mom told Laurie, "Whatever you're holding comes with you when you die," before grasping hold of her, sputtering, and rolling her eyes back in her head.

The thing is, when family members weren't pretending to die, for gags, they were doing it for real, kicking off the litany of traumas that punctuated the punch lines. Ronnie, Mom's older brother, is struck by a vehicle and killed at age four; a few years later, her dad, my grandpa, dies at thirty-three from a heart condition, not only plunging the family into fatherlessness but also causing a precipitous drop in socio-economic standing from a family headed by a wealthy, hotshot young lawyer to one led by a widowed mother; at age twenty, the baby of the family, my uncle Chris, is run over by a car while riding his bicycle; three years after that, my mother is diagnosed with leukemia, and she dies a few years later, in the house that my parents, my brother and I share with my granny and auntie Heather, while we are all at home. I am ten years old.

So those are the pitch-black opening credits that roll before the sitcom of my maternal family's life. I see them ending with the Grim Reaper in the role of wacky neighbour, giving the camera a "Whaddya gonna do?" shrug while a bucket of water or something falls on his head, or he notices one of those pesky Birnie kids has replaced his scythe with a goalie stick.

I think those traumas produced the rapid alternation between grief and laughter that marks my family, and defines them for me. It's probably the way in which I feel most deeply and irrevocably a part of the family, too.

*   *   *

What can humour do?

Well, who among us can forget the great Smarm versus Snark wars of late 2013? They began when *Gawker* contributor Tom Scocca wrote a terrific essay defending the snipey, caustically ironic sensibility widely denounced as "snark" against what he saw as the sententious, self-righteous faux-positivity of the powerful and privileged, identified as "smarm." The piece called out bestselling author, speaker and *New Yorker* essayist Malcolm Gladwell as a prime purveyor of said smarm, so unsurprisingly came in for a strong (and, dare I say it, somewhat smarmy) rebuttal from him. Gladwell cherry-picked quotes from Scocca's piece that made him seem humourless and wildly unpleasant, then proceeded to cite another of the year's remarkable essays—this one a brilliantly argued and thoroughly depressing meditation by Jonathan Coe in the *London Review of Books* on the limits of political satire. "It's not the respectful voice that props up the status quo," wrote Gladwell, channelling Coe, "it is the mocking one."

I had read Coe's piece, "Sinking Giggling into the Sea," when it came out and, as a politically minded comedian, had been winded by it. I'd winced through sentence after sentence like the following: "Famously, when opening his club, The Establishment, in Soho in 1961, [Peter] Cook remarked that he was modelling it on 'those wonderful Berlin cabarets which did so much to stop the rise of Hitler and prevent the outbreak of the Second World War.'" *Dude.* Fucking *ouch*, dude.

The question of what humour can and can't do to subvert or protect us from that which terrifies us and oppresses us, in either our political or our personal lives, is an open one. Can a tyranny be toppled in a Chaplinesque pratfall? Or does laughter anaesthetize us against injustice? Can finding humour in the dark corners of our lives give us the strength to confront what's hurting us? Or does it let us run away from our own problems and adopt a callous attitude to those of other people? The answer, as in virtually every cheesy, rhetorical, straw-man dichotomy like the ones I've just set up, is both and neither.

When my friend Bill and his fiancée were visiting her mother, who was in the last stages of cancer and running constantly to the bathroom to vomit, he turned to his beloved with a look of deep concern on his face and said, "Do you think she might be bulimic?" Now: Is that one of the most tasteless jokes ever made by anyone I know? Absolutely (and I'm a stand-up comic, so please believe me when I tell you that is saying something). Would Bill be a horrible person if that were all he ever offered, emotionally, in life's difficult spots? Most certainly. But was his fiancée forever grateful for the gust of air that his gallows levity had let into the room? Would I be relating this story here if she hadn't been?

Ultimately, I think the philosopher Simon Critchley gets it right, in his book *On Humour* (those academics and their inscrutable titles!): "Humour does not redeem us from this world, but returns us to it ineluctably by showing that there is no alternative. The consolations of humour come from acknowledging that this is the only world and, imperfect as it is and we are, it is only here that we can make a difference." In other words, every time a lounge act tells you "I'm here all week, try the veal," he's reminding you we're all mortal, and furthermore, there are little baby cows being kept in tiny cages, so what are you going to do about that?

*　　*　　*

Life is terrible—politically, socially, personally—and it's hilarious, and it is in that spirit that I offer the following essays. I have endeavoured to write something at least a little bit funny inspired by one terrible thing for every letter of the alphabet. Some are big-picture social things, like "C for Capitalism" or "U for Union-Busting"; others skew far more personal, like "F for Fat" and "D for Depression." Some deal with minor irritants, like when stand-up comedy goes badly in "B for Bombing," whereas others treat the hardest things I've ever experienced, such as

"O for Obsessive-Compulsive Disorder" and "M for Motherlessness." Some names have been changed, in case anybody (other than me) should be embarrassed.

I chose the alphabet as a frame for a couple of reasons. For starters, as anyone who's read Edward Gorey's *The Gashlycrumb Tinies* will avow, you can afford to get pretty dark while playing inside the alphabet because it takes the edge off; the alphabet brings us back to childhood. As a new father, I have read and enjoyed more than a few ABC books over the past year (unlike when I read my daughter *The Little Engine That Could* once and, in a moment remembered with equal parts shame and irony, gave up halfway). But even before becoming a dad, I always enjoyed abecedarian collections, like the several written by my friend George Bowering. We were talking once about ABC books and George said something along the lines of, "I can't remember who said this, me or Roland Barthes, but the great thing about the alphabet is that it's a totally random order, but everybody knows it." In the end, that's my favourite reason for using it. And for the record, one of my own humble little goals in life is to reach a level of accomplishment where I, too, can pretend to confuse my own musings with those of Roland Barthes.

for Adolescence

THE VERY FIRST TIME I brought myself to climax in a waking state was: (a) by accident, (b) on Halloween, (c) to Sarah Jessica Parker in the Disney film *Hocus Pocus* and (d) at the age of sixteen. Unfortunately, these are not multiple-choice answers to a question that no one would ever ask; this is a list of simple irrefutable facts. Now listen, I know that readers, especially female ones, will be induced to catatonic boredom by yet another rendering of that most literarily privileged of rites, the onanistic quest for male sexual pleasure—and I'm sympathetic to that boredom, so I won't dwell on the subject. Nevertheless, that's what happened, and I'm stuck with it, and furthermore, if you asked me to pick the hard kernel at the centre of my experience of teenage becoming—that terrifying, flailing attempt, at adulthood's doorstep, to come to grips with one's social, intellectual and physical self—I'd be lying if I were to locate it somewhere other than in that lunatic knot of facts.

So many of the totally unanswerable questions typical of adolescence are bound up in that moment: Why wasn't I at a Halloween party? Or watching a scary movie with friends? Or outside setting off Roman candles? Why a PG-rated movie from Disney, when home internet had so recently brought all the ways of the flesh right into the suburban home? Why had I never done it before then, and even then why did I do it with such shame that I set myself off without meaning to? I had grown up in an open-minded, forward-thinking household, where books and a loving father assured and reassured me that self-pleasure was natural and universal—but I never believed any if it for a minute. In fact, I was emboldened enough to go back for a second go at the experience only after a schoolmate had sheepishly offered, in the course of another conversation altogether, "Well... Every guy has *tried* it..." Why was I so remedial as to be losing my masturbatory virginity just as my peers were losing their actual virginities—even though I had bolted past most of them polit-ically and intellectually, harbouring by then relatively informed opinions on Quebec independence, the occupation of Palestine and the Russian Revolution?

As it turns out, that seeming contradiction is not so much a paradox as an explanation. Generally speaking, the adolescent is a person setting off on the beginning of both conscious intellec-tual life and romantic, sexual life—and although the two usual-ly unfold more or less in step with each other, in my case the one cut the other off, like those fetuses you read about that kill and absorb their twins. In fact, I can trace the entire process back to one night.

The groundwork was laid for my recruitment into the inter-national communist movement at the age of fifteen, on what happened to be the evening of my very first kiss. In retrospect, it's fitting that both my sexual career and my career as an anti-capitalist revolutionary began on the same night, as each has been roughly as successful as the other. It was the spring of 1996, and I was at work on two things, neither of which was particu-larly surprising or counterintuitive for a chubby, precocious sub-urban teenage boy: I was in the school play, and I was reading *The Communist Manifesto* for the first time.

I was then, as I am now, someone who projected more intelli-gence than he actually possessed, so my reading the *Manifesto* was something a fairly large group of people knew about (even though reading is usually a pretty quiet, solitary pursuit) and also seemed to last a very long time (even though the *Manifesto* is a pretty short book). I plodded through Marx and Engels's bullet-speed survey of world history as a series of class struggles at the same time as and with the same dexterity with which I plodded through increasingly reciprocated flirtations with Meghan, a very sweet and beautiful freckled girl who was also in the play. Unlike humanity's march through slavery, feudalism and capitalism, our attraction was non-dialectical: it was soft and sweet, and I had the strong intuition—as it turns out, correct—that we would give in to our mutual urges and attractions at the wrap party for the show.

The get-together was hosted by a punk rock kid named Mike who had played a small part in the production. As the cast and crew entered his house after our last curtain call, he presented us all to his parents. We got quick introductions, delivered in just the amount of time it took to remove one's shoes, and since all I could think about was Meghan, who had been *holding my hand* on the walk over from the theatre, it barely even registered when it was my turn to be presented to Mom and Dad. Mike said: "This is Chuck. He has a communist book." I went downstairs with the other kids, smoked a joint in the carport to build up my courage, then went inside to sit with my almost-possibly girlfriend.

In my daydreams of how the moment would go, Meghan would start things by giving me an innocent little peck, and then I would say, in a deep voice that my testicles hadn't yet given me, "Did you just kiss me?" to which she would nod bashfully, and then I, full of confidence, would say, "Well, then I should kiss you back," immediately before the passion began. Now, socialists in general are very good at imagining fantastical, ideal historical conditions magically coming about and allowing them to realize their goals, and basically that never happens. But on this night, everything went according to my utopian blueprint. Well, except for the confidence part—I probably stopped Meghan four or five times to ask if I was kissing her properly. Otherwise, though, and unbelievably, I was having my first kiss exactly how I dreamed it would be, except for one other detail: in imagining what my first make-out session would be like, I had never once imagined that the whole time, just ten feet above me, there'd be two middle-aged Trotskyists rubbing their hands together about the fact that I was reading a communist book.

As it turns out, Mike's parents, Dale and Linda, were active supporters of a party called the Communist League (CL), made up mostly of white, formerly lower-middle-class people turned blue-collar workers, the majority of whom had joined the movement because of their opposition to the Vietnam War. The party members' rapid aging and not-so-rapid reproduction helped explain why they'd be so chuffed about a teenager reading the *Manifesto*—they were always looking to recruit new members to their youth wing, the Young Socialists (YS). The Communist League was the Canadian counterpart to the American Socialist Workers Party (SWP), a sect led by a man named Jack in New York. Jack spoke in a voice not unlike Ross Perot's, and although he was missing his left arm, he would gesticulate wildly with it during interminable speeches (I promise this is true and not the worst possible metaphoric device for fleshing out the leader of a struggling socialist party). The CL and the SWP put out a week-ly communist newspaper called the *Militant,* and every week, at affiliated bookstores across the continent, hosted public talks called the Militant Labor Forum. Well—*theoretically* public. As you can imagine, people weren't hammering down the doors to get in.

Mike turned up at school the day after the party with a yellow, photocopied notice for an upcoming Friday-night forum, with a kind handwritten invitation from his parents on the back. And although my approximately month-long romance with Meghan would come to include several well-planned romantic even-ings (like the night we watched TV together in my dad's room, or the evening we went to see Uma Thurman and Janeane Garo-falo's *The Truth About Cats & Dogs)*, my very first Friday with a

girlfriend was spent not in her presence, but rather at the Pathfinder Bookstore—whose name, suggestive of either religious inclination or some sort of affiliation with Nissan, belied the revolutionary excitement within.

There are very few adventures in the life of a fifteen-year-
old, lower-middle-class white boy in western Canada. In a world
where the forces of commerce have absorbed everything that's
been thrown at them—I mean, the first punk rock show I ever
saw was in an arena, for Christ's sake—there are so few experi-
ences that feel genuinely *outside* of everything else. By this definition, my first visit to the Pathfinder Bookstore was an adventure.

There was a casual atmosphere, with people eating off paper
plates; there'd been a fundraising dinner before the forum that
evening. The titles of the books on the shelves were thrilling: *Imperialism's March Toward Fascism and War. Art and Revolution*.
Nelson Mandela and Fidel Castro, arms around each other, smiling under the title *How Far We Slaves Have Come!* Even more incredible, even more outside of things, was everyone using words
like "comrade," and "socialist," and "communist." *Communist*.
They were proud of it. This word I had heard a thousand times,
in movies and on TV, always meaning something bad and rotten, someone evil, but within these walls was the best thing you
could call somebody. The way they used the word was attractive, charismatic. In retrospect, it's easy to see why: it was disorienting. If some dude came up to you and said: "Yeah, I'm a
douchebag, I love being a douchebag, I'm proud to be a part of
the long douchebag heritage," a large part of you would think,
What does this guy know that I don't? The way they said "communist" put them outside the End of History era I'd grown up
in, the liberal capitalism everybody seemed to agree was now
the only option for how to organize society. Instead, they articu-
lated their position within living history with such confidence,
offering an identity that seemed so solid and indissoluble in the
acid of the free market, in the rest of everyday life, that they
drew me in.

It had to be something like that that made me stick around—
the members of the CL weren't exactly all-stars of charisma on
their own. I seem to remember that speaking with one's mouth
full was a shared challenge—I dodged bits of pita bread and bas-
mati rice during emphatic dialogues with more than one comrade over the years.

The big cheese in the local branch of the party was Stan, who
arrived from Toronto just a few months after I'd started hanging
around the bookstore. There was a sense of occasion when he
landed, with his wife, Marie, from the big city. Stan came from
a notable Canadian Communist family—Stalinist, pro-Soviet,
capital-C Communist; Stan's Trotskyism was how one rebelled
in a family of rebels. Silver-haired, silver-bearded, Stan looked
and spoke like a tenured professor, with two differences: he was
constantly drinking chocolate milk, and he was clearly lactose
intolerant. Stan had an elegant inelegance about him—an anti-
charm that made him the centre of the room. He spoke with a
stutter, but it never diminished his authority. It became a poised
stammer; in fact, years later, Barack Obama would adopt a Stan-
like staccato to give his speeches gravitas. Stan would sit with his
legs tightly crossed and a heavy-lidded expression, making casual, almost dismissive waves of his open palm, holding forth with
infinite confidence on a particular uprising or a particular labour
action, when he would let out a fart unacknowledged by anyone or anything besides the sound waves careening through the
room. Stan was finely attuned to every hotspot of struggle and
turmoil on earth, except inside his own intestinal tract. I don't
know if you've ever heard a middle-aged man fart through cor-
duroy pants onto a metal chair seventeen times in a row during
a presentation on the necessity of Puerto Rican independence,
but it's something.

For the next three years of my life, the rest of my adolescence,
only the Young Socialists mattered to me. That night of my first
kiss, the night of the wrap party, two doors had been opened to
me: one to the world of romance, and possibly sex. The other into

the world of anti-capitalist, left-wing politics. Like a schmuck, I took the second one. Eventually, several pals would join me in the ranks of the revolution, but social relations with non-comrades became secondary. I didn't attend parties, because the YS's "security policy" prohibited being anyplace where illegal drugs were present (otherwise the state could use its drug laws to sabotage the revolutionary movement, *duh*—and yes, for careful readers, this does mean that the carport joint on the evening of my first kiss could've landed Dale and Linda in serious trouble). Friday nights were for forums; Saturdays were for literature tables, where we would hawk books and newspapers to an indifferent public like anti-capitalist Jehovah's Witnesses; Sundays were for reading groups, YS meetings, discussions. I became the Doogie Howser of the party: I was flown down to San Francisco to deliver a Militant Labor Forum about Quebec, in the Mission District; I was writing articles for the *Militant,* sometimes under a pseudonym. My dream became to move to New York and write full time for the paper at subsistence wages, as I had heard that some comrades were lucky enough to get to do.

Somehow, though, my infatuation with the party was coterminous with my being a teenager. As high school ended, it was time for me to matriculate from the Young Socialists into the Communist League itself and become what we called a "worker-Bolshevik." Since in our reading of Marxist doctrine only the industrial working class could successfully overthrow capitalism, it behooved each and every comrade to be a member of it. As the summer of my eighteenth birthday rolled around, and most of the people I knew were getting ready to go off to university, I submitted a resumé full of lies to a prepackaged furniture factory in the suburbs, where a few other comrades were working and where we could form what was called a "fraction"—a workplace cell of revolutionaries. I turned eighteen years old, got steel-toed boots and began my miserable life of worker-Bolshevism.

Or, more accurately, Sisyphean-Leninism: a day might begin, at five in the morning, with driving out to the boonies for a "plant-gate sale," which in theory meant standing outside a factory and selling the newspaper to workers as they went in for the morning shift but in practice meant standing outside a factory, in ·pitch-black, freezing-cold darkness, as bemused and half-asleep workers drove past you without giving you a second thought, besides maybe, *Just who in the fuck are those lunatics?*

After selling zero papers at the plant gate, it was time to go into the factory, where you yourself worked, putting in a gruelling eight-, nine- or twelve-hour shift. You couldn't come out as a communist or whip out the *Militant* in the lunchroom during your three-month probation. As a result, no one else at work knew that those nutty old revolutionaries—the lazy old grey-bearded men who probably should have been professors but were instead grinding aluminum caps for lighting fixtures and could be found taking unauthorized breaks in the washroom, leaning up against the cubicle walls trying to catch their breath—were your comrades. So you'd hear, straight from the proletarian's mouth, just how batshit crazy everyone thought they, and by extension you, were. The whole time, of course, I knew that once I got off probation, I would have to do plant-gate sales outside my own factory. I was pre-emptively mortified.

Evenings after work were spent in meetings, where comrades became a bit less guarded with the crazy than they had been when I was just in the YS. I showed up late to a special conference once and was put on trial for it. I can't say that, at the time, I fully appreciated the insanity of a group of fiftysomethings holding a trial for an eighteen-year-old who showed up fifteen minutes late to a meeting—but I wasn't an idiot, either. Part of me knew it was bananas. Then one day, on the factory floor, in the midst of one of my normal mindless tasks, the light changed on the scene and, suddenly, I felt an almost uncontrollable sadness. I saw the enormous length of my life, my one life, rolling out ahead of me, filled with nothing but the worst work available and endless meetings full of loud, unexcused flatulence. I gave up and wrote a self-flagellating letter of resignation, retiring forever as a worker-Bolshevik.

The temptation, of course, in sharing a story like this is to lean towards complete ridicule and disavowal, landing some-place age-appropriately conservative: "Wow, what a bunch of left-wing lunatics. Ergo, capitalism is the greatest." But that's not really how adolescence works. Our teenage years—crazy, embar-rassing and painful as they are—seem to me to be where we in-cubate our adulthood, trying out a crazier, more extreme, more awkward version of the grown-ups we're going to be. As silly and as distant as so much of it seems in retrospect, I still have to admit I learned a lot in those years, and vestigial elements of the revolutionary virgin that I was in those days are still with me. Halfway through my thirties, Meghan and I are still friends, and I remain a committed socialist—if of a markedly less incendi-ary pedigree than I once was. And all the indications seem to be that the sight of Sarah Jessica Parker dressed up like a witch, rid-ing a broom, will warm my cold October nights until the end of my days.

B for BOMBING

for Bombing

To BEGIN, LET'S clarify terms: in this essay, "bombing" will be used in the vernacular sense of a comedian's badly failing in front of a hostile or indifferent crowd of (usually) drunks, rather than in the death-from-above, carnage-on-the-ground geopolitical usage. I feel eminently qualified to discuss the former, having had, as a stand-up comic, my fair share of failure in front of hostile or indifferent crowds of (usually) drunks. Contrarily, living in the safe little corner of the world from which missiles are almost always launched but in which they're never expected to land, I don't think it's my place to try to find the "lighter side" of be-rubbling far-flung neighbourhoods. Even the things that *are* funny about that kind of bombing—say, that the lion's share of Western pundits and policymakers seem to think that it offers a perfectly plausible road towards feminist liberation, democratic stability and flowering free market prosperity in the more deeply tanned regions of the world—aren't so much ha-ha funny as weep-for-the-state-of-humanity funny.

So, stand-up. Stand-up comedy is a little bit like working in a soup kitchen on Christmas—okay, only a *very little* bit like that, and only in the sense that the number of people who've actually done it is tiny in relation to the number of people who've thought about trying it or, more importantly, make a point of letting others know that they've thought about trying it. Like getting more into jazz music or voting for the Green Party, just the thought of doing stand-up, without any follow-through, seems to scratch the itch it's supposed to. I imagine that in their fantasy version of how it might go most people see themselves taking to the stage for the first time and effortlessly unloading a barrage of witticisms unprecedented in their trenchancy, power and originality, collapsing the crowd into helpless peels of laughter.

The allure of this vision, however, doesn't seem to be enough to risk their apocalypse-scenario version of how it might play out: a crowd of furrowed brows, a collective rictus of amazed lack of enjoyment, the suffocating silence at the end of every punch line. They are afraid, in short, of bombing. Underneath the YouTube video "'COMIC' BOMBS, BREAKS DOWN, DIES ON-STAGE!!!" in which a male comedian who uses the term "friend-zone" seven times in the first minute of his set finds it impossible to connect with a New York crowd, someone has commented, "I'm doing stand up comedy soon and this is my worst nightmare."

For this reason, in the odd but not unheard-of event that I am asked for advice by someone setting out to try stand-up for the first time, my suggestion is always that they get onstage quickly to get the experience out of the way and that above all else they moderate their expectations of how things will go. There will not be laurels or ovations, nor will the crowd want to see them fail. It's good advice, generally.

It's the advice I gave several years ago in the green room of a Yuk Yuk's comedy club when I was hosting an amateur night and looking into the eyes of two would-be comics about to try things out for the first time—one, a very small attractive woman with dark hair and eyes; the other, a tall and oppressively jocular grey-haired man who looked like he had once been very beautiful. After taking my counsel—you're not going to bring them to their feet, but you're not going to bomb—the man went out through the thick red velveteen curtains and performed what

was, without question, one of the poorest and most poorly received sets I've ever witnessed. Wall to wall, it was as it must have
been in his very worst nightmares. The only joke that I remember went generally as follows (with my annotations in square
brackets): "'Fellatio' [Are you excited about the joke yet? Fresh
territory!], that's a funny word, isn't it? [Only vaguely. Where are
you going with this?] It sounds like a boy's name. [No, not re-
motely] 'Come here, Fellatio!' [Oof.]" This last line was accompanied by what we in the business call an "act out," in this case
involving the comic pantomiming his invitation of the young and
unfortunately named Fellatio's face into his crotch, before muss-
ing the mop of his imaginary hair. The man came backstage vis-
ibly shaken, his face drained of all blood and will to live, just as
the young woman went out for her set—and absolutely brought
the house down, with several applause breaks, every single joke
landing as though she were taping an HBO special. In the end,
she stuck around doing stand-up for several years; I never saw
Fellatio's progenitor again. So, okay—I don't know everything.
Nevertheless, I maintain that my advice for first-timers is *generally* pretty good.

There is no cultural métier in which a person fails more
fluorescently than in comedy, besides maybe trapeze acrobatics. And as with trapeze acrobatics, although there is nothing
so chest-heatingly terrible as watching someone fail at comedy,
when it happens it is hypnotic—you can't turn away, and you're
ashamed of the part of you that thinks, *This is far more compelling than if things had gone well.* "'COMIC' BOMBS, BREAKS
DOWN, DIES ON-STAGE!!!" has 100,024 views—a large number
itself but dwarfed by the 2,316,986 who've watched the excruciating "Comedian Boo Off Stage," which begins with the comic
receiving applause for the opening line, "First of all I gotta stop
and give honour to God, because without Him I would not be
here today" but ends with the evening's emcee announcing from
the stage, "N*gga, you ain't going to get no pussy tonight" and an
audience member screaming, "Hell, no!"

The reason failure in comedy is so much more obvious than in other forms is that, like a marriage proposal, there is only one possible positive outcome for a joke, and when that's not what happens, there is no hiding it. If, say, the underperforming (or underperformed) melodies of a live band fail to entice an audience into sweaty, passionate dance, then quiet, contemplative "active listening" can be faked; if the meaning of a particularly inscrutable piece of poetry or abstract art continues to evade, a reasonable facsimile of silent, knowing comprehension can usually be performed. Not so with the dread silence of an audience not laughing. Occasionally, a desperate club manager or fellow performer will reassure the comic that "Everybody's really listening, and they're all smiling." Somehow, that's worse.

I remember watching, years ago, a struggling stand-up comedian on the *Late Show with David Letterman.* In the midst of what this guy had certainly been hoping would be his break—the moment after which everything would be demonstrably different, and better—joke after joke failed to land. Without losing his smile, his eyes began to search, plead. It was pure misery. The incredible thing was you could somehow tell by listening to the audience that they wanted just as desperately as he did for them to laugh. They *liked* him, they were *unanimously* pulling for him, but they were powerless to help until he gave them something they could genuinely laugh at. Finally, his closer—a bit about cars with their horns on a little wand spoking out from the steering wheel as opposed to being in the centre of the steering wheel itself and what a rip-off they were, because, now, if you got shot and slumped over in the driver's seat, it wouldn't make a sound—erupted the crowd into an elated release completely out of proportion to the rest of the act.

Bombing a TV taping, especially one as important as *Letterman,* is as bad as bombing gets. Otherwise, it's tough to say for whom it's worse: amateurs or practising professionals. A pro can take comfort in a (hopefully) long string of past successes that came before whatever she happens to be enduring in the moment; there can even be a certain bemused, cocky delight in seeing a joke that's succeeded two hundred times before fall flat for once—it's a novelty, and after all, the comedian has close to empirically verifiable data that it's not her, or the joke, but rather that night's crowd. Amateurs have no similar body of work to weigh painful moments against; their entire sense of self is freshly on the block with every premise and punch line.

But unlike amateurs, who at least know that they can leave at any time, a professional is contractually obligated to stay onstage telling more jokes for a certain number of minutes. There are few worse feelings in the non-tragic human repertoire. To extend the question-popping analogy: standing in front of a crowd that evidently hates you and knowing you have to continue to try to make them laugh is like being legally required to continue trying to flirt with someone who has just rejected your Jumbotron proposal at a football game.

The first time I can remember bombing at a paid gig seems, in retrospect, to have been lab-engineered for failure. A few of us were performing after dinner in the upstairs banquet hall of the Royal Vancouver Yacht Club for the staff of a local janitorial service and supply franchise. The host and organizer of the show informed me that the occasion for the special dinner was the introduction of a new soap. My bafflingly obscure opening line—"Sani-Service, I haven't been this excited about a new soap since *Fight Club!*"—drew not indifference (which would have been painful enough) but genuine confused disgust. Unlike in a comedy club, where the lighting works at least to camouflage the audience's distaste in darkness, the room at the yacht club was fully lit, so I could see each and every audience member's face twisting in angry, aghast bewilderment. They were emoting like extras trying to win an Academy Award. After my set, I returned humiliated to my seat. The host was now introducing the next act, a very funny guy with whom I was friendly but who I now silently begged the universe would also fail miserably, so that I could say "it was the crowd." Post-show, wound-licking solidarity after a gig that doesn't go well for anybody is a balm against the effects of bombing—each of us bands together to heap gleeful sour grapes scorn on the dumb audience that clearly wasn't there to laugh, was unreachable.

Alas, not Sani-Service. They thrilled to the next act, who seemed to be growing taller right in front of us. Jokes, sound effects, impressions—the crowd nearly lost its collective mind as he imitated, uncannily, his alcoholic jazz musician Irish uncle puking through a saxophone. He came back to sit with me anointed. Success in comedy is just as unambiguous as failure. And side by side, they're so unambiguous you want to cry.

If there is comfort to be found in the face of bombing, it is to be drawn from its inevitability. In an impassioned video, also on YouTube, legendary comedy manager-producer George Shapiro explains the necessity of bombing in the comedian's development as an inextricable component of the artistic process: "You have to embrace it," he urges. "You'll be in pain, you'll feel terrible—I've seen comedians crying after. I've seen comedians very upset. But the ones that really have made it—they've all bombed. Every comedian bombs. Every comedian. They have to." He continues to give an explanation of the way it works, the role it plays, which in effect adds up to a moving tribute to human imperfection and to the basic, beautiful creative impulse towards elusive aesthetic perfection. It has a little more than one thousand views.

C for CAPITALISM

for Capitalism

I WAS BORN AT the same time as the deregulated free market, and in both my life and the life of unfettered capitalism, it's only now, after all these years, that we can look back and try to piece together how everything went so wrong.

I was born on July 1, 1980, and for my darling mother this augured well—not only personally but politically. My mom saw a great deal of auspiciousness in the date of my birth and in its attendant symbolism: it was Canada Day, just six weeks after Quebec had voted to stay in the country (for the first time, anyway), and here I was, being born on the national holiday (even though I'd been due on American Independence Day), to an English-speaking mother and a Québécois father. It seemed that I *was* Canada—although the analogy isn't perfect, because my folks didn't steal the delivery room from an Indigenous family that was already using it.

Nevertheless, my mom had high hopes that all of this meant that I, her first-born son, would one day be the country's prime minister. And in the imagination of my mother, who was a deeply religious, generous-of-spirit Christian, a Tommy Douglas–type Christian, I would inevitably be the kind of prime minister who would orchestrate generosity and solidarity, shepherding a society wherein people looked out for one another and where the amassing of grotesque private fortunes would always be distantly secondary to meeting the material and spiritual needs of the common person. You know, an *imaginary* prime minister.

In fairness, that kind of illusion was understandable for a person in my mother's historical situation: being a white, anglophone woman born in North America six years after World War II ended into an era of egalitarian redistribution and reorganization unprecedented in human history. All of it had specific political roots, of course—the previously unimaginable power of organized labour and anti-colonial movements, the anti-fascist coalitions that had won the war and beaten back the Depression, the sense of communal well-being wrought by *It's a Wonderful Life,* the socially cohesive effects of sock hops... But for a generation of baby boomers like my mom, in her part of the world, anyway, and of her cultural background, this wave of egalitarianism signalled the new direction in which humanity was moving, and why on earth would that ever cease to be the case?

She didn't realize that by the time her son was born—she'd gotten pregnant six months after Margaret Thatcher was elected prime minister of Britain and given birth five months before Ronald Reagan was elected president of the United States—that historical moment had already passed. For almost two hundred years before her son came along, since the time of the French Revolution at least, a significant and serious segment of the world population had believed that society could, should and (most incredibly, in retrospect) probably *would* be upended, seized from the rich and powerful and improved for the sake of the poor, oppressed and working classes. But my mom had no way of knowing that she had given birth at almost exactly the same moment that pretty much everybody but crazy people and tenured academics stopped believing that. It was a post-utopian postpartum; as a child of the 1980s, the soundtrack I grew up with was dominated by the two Tinas: Ms. Turner and the acronym from the Lady who wasn't for turning—Mrs. Thatcher's insistence "There is no alternative." Now, we were all just private dancers. Dancers for money.

Reagan and Thatcher had been elected expressly to roll back the post-war reality that my mother had come up in (not like a personal vendetta against my mother, of course; I just mean in general). They beat back the unions, drove down wages, cut taxes for the very rich and scaled back the regulatory power of the state. Around the same time, Deng Xiaoping was working in Communist China towards liberalizing markets, and similar market-liberating goals were animating the Central American death squads (often funded by only partially free markets in snortable commodities). Interest rates around the world were cranked up, French prime minister François Mitterrand abandoned his socialist campaign pledges in the face of the bond markets and the stand-up comedy of Yakov Smirnoff left the Eastern Bloc ideologically reeling from a cascade of comic misdirections and sentence inversions.

The capitalist euphoria of the early '80s even trickled down—in one of the only proven cases of trickle-down ever working—to the book-buying public. The number two *New York Times* non-fiction bestseller the week I was born was *Free to Choose*, a paean to the spirit of capitalism and the single-minded pursuit of profit unhindered by the weight of a calcified interventionist government, written by husband and wife monetarist economists Milton and Rose Friedman. Now, you may be thinking, *Well, number two isn't number one,* but in fairness, the number one book the week I was born was a Gay Talese title about sex, and it can be difficult to compete with sex, especially when the cover of your book is a giant picture of Milton Friedman holding a pencil, making it the exact opposite of sex. (Despite having co-authored the book with Rose, Milton appears stag on the cover, suggesting he was such a big fan of the invisible hand that he went one further and found himself an invisible bride.)

In the first moments of the pilot episode of *The Sopranos*, HBO's magisterial tragicomedy about capitalism by other means, lumbering Tony tells his brand-new therapist, "It's good to be in something from the ground floor. I came in too late for that, I know. But lately, I'm getting the feeling that I came in at the end. The best is over." Tony's talking about the mob, and he's talking about the United States of America, but with barely any tweaking, the line could just as easily be uttered by an anti-capitalist born after—or, in my case, in the course of—1980, socialism's equivalent of the Mayans' apocalyptic 2012. In any discussion of how rotten and vastly unequal our societies have become, the year of my birth keeps coming up like an expiration date on a carton of lumpy milk: lefty economist Linda McQuaig compares "the enormous concentration of income and wealth after 1980" with the pre-Depression roar of the 1920s; the social democratic historian Tony Judt cited the lamentations of his young students, who complained to him that "you [baby boomers] were able to change things. 'We' (the children of the '80s, the '90s, the 'aughts') have nothing. In many respects my students are right." The year the now-proverbial 1 percent began stacking up their lion's share of newly created wealth was the same year that I, future socialist prime minister of Canada, began stacking blocks.

The term used by some free-market cheerleaders for the era in which my peers and I were brought up was the "End of History"—which, despite being a stark and terrifying phrase, was supposed to be a good thing, a pin-striped version of when nutty Evangelicals describe the screaming hellfire of Armageddon, before giddily telling you they can't wait for it. The first nine years of my life were the last of what's called the "short twentieth century": 1914–89, an epoch defined by a number of things; it would be silly to try to reduce it to just one dynamic, but challenges to capitalism as the only way of doing things were certainly among its more salient features, alongside the Beatles. Experiments in social democracy and communism were carried out all over the world, with both modes of non-capitalist governance producing some remarkable achievements as well as terrible missteps and more than a soupçon of murderous atrocity. But the End of

History meant that these types of experiments were now over. We had found the best, and therefore only, way of doing things: liberal democratic capitalism. With a special emphasis on that last part.

The happy days of the End of History, with genuinely repellent regimes in the Eastern Bloc being brought low along with the Berlin Wall, were something like the last moments of *The Graduate*—humanity runs giggling breathlessly onto a bus, hand in hand with the dynamic capitalism that just saved us from miserable unfreedom, before sinking into a deep ambivalence about our prospects. Except that in the free market version of *The Graduate*, there wouldn't have been a publicly funded municipal bus to board, and the real hero of the movie would've been the guy who was so excited about plastics.

My mother lived to see the end of the Cold War and the collapse of Communism, but just barely. She had developed leukemia in 1986, when I was five and a half years old, and she would be in the hospital for weeks-long stretches throughout my childhood. I was made aware, even as a kid, that there was an arrangement in our country whereby we didn't have to pay directly for the expensive medicine and treatment that Mom was receiving, and that we couldn't have paid for it if there weren't. It was one of those old and dying twentieth-century ideas. That sort of arrangement, our family didn't yet realize, was just one more government bulwark against liberty and efficiency, a distortion of price signals and the glory of competition, disrupting the sort of unfettered trade that was going to turn the world into a community of nations now that the Cold War was over. At the end of January 1991, President George Herbert Walker Bush gave his State of the Union address and called for the establishment of a "new world order" ("new world order" is one of those phrases, like "military-industrial complex," that you forget was coined by a U.S. president because you only ever hear conspiracy theorists use it). Bush was talking about Operation Desert Storm, and my memories of the First Gulf War are inextricably bound up with my last memories of my mother.

As I would come to learn, the big difference between a mother, on the one hand, and on the other, a president Bush or a war in Iraq, is that with mothers you only get one. A month and a half after the "new world order" speech, on March 11, 1991, I lost mine. By the end, I don't know if she still thought, or hoped, I would lead the federal government one day. Truth be told, I don't know if that was ever for real; I just think it was the kind of sweet thing a person says as they're holding their little baby. Whatever the case, the year she died was the same one in which the Union of Soviet Socialist Republics dissolved itself. Over the course of the next few years, Russia would have thrust upon it a newly energized and rapacious form of capitalism, while on the other side of the world, I, my mother's first-born son, was voted by the 1998 graduating class of Burnaby Central Secondary School the student most likely to become prime minister.

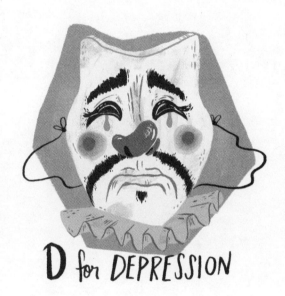

D for DEPRESSION

for Depression

ONE OF THE FIRST jokes I ever told onstage, when I had just started doing stand-up comedy, was about selective serotonin reuptake inhibitors, or SSRIs. The bit went: "My doctor gave me a prescription for antidepressants, and as he was doling them out he said to me, 'Be careful with these—they aren't Tic Tacs,' so I roll my eyes and say 'Right, like I'd ever take *fifteen* Tic Tacs.'" The joke isn't superb, but it isn't terrible, and given that I was a young male brand new to doing stand-up, the fact that it wasn't a nervously hateful joke about prison rape makes it almost miraculous. I was also following the old injunction to "write what you know."

I was, at the time, successfully pursuing a course of antidepressants, specifically citalopram, the Canadian generic of the drug called Celexa (try to imagine a phrase more evocative of depression than "Canadian generic"). Citalopram/Celexa had been my second—and desperate—shot at SSRIs, and I took it, to good effect, for several years, only deciding to get off it on the week of my honeymoon. This may or may not have been a good idea; that was the same week that I decided to go on the Atkins diet, so I certainly wasn't batting a thousand in terms of life choices at the time.

One of the most cherished paradoxes in our society—certainly, at least, among the writers of lazy celebrity profiles—is that supposedly the very people who make the world laugh and bring everyone joy are, get this... *the saddest of all*! The appeal of the myth runs both ways: for the purveyors of it, it makes for an easy, instantly compelling story that one doesn't need to do any work or have any insight to find and shape; for the comedians, it brings a moody gravitas to an otherwise goofy life's work, or even life. It's also an incongruity, and comedians are most comfortable with the incongruous. All in all, it's a "man bites dog, also has seven pretty solid minutes of dog material" type of story.

It's a narrative, though, of limited accuracy and usefulness. For starters, it's only really true of one type of comedian. Go spend some time with improv comics—you will find they possess next to no guile or dark irony and more *joie de vivre* and *esprit de corps* than a book of French phrases; there is a level of trust and happiness among improv comics suggestive of a religious cult. Sketch comedians, too, are in my experience an army of smiling competence, working together offstage to craft content like grown-ups, then playing together under the lights with the spiritual transcendence of children.

This leaves only stand-up comedians to bear Pagliacci's burden (or standard), and granted, the ranks of stand-ups are indeed infinitely mopier, more darkly cruel and more toxic than those of our sketch and improv colleagues. Go to a comedy festival sometime and watch stand-ups trying to converse with sketch and improv people—it's like watching a thread unfold on your Facebook page between your pie-baking friends from church choir and the flaking, pale-faced guys you met at an auto-erotic asphyxiation clinic.

That said, there is certainly a selection bias at work among the miserable stand-ups, given that ours is a trade practically designed to accommodate, soothe or incentivize depressive symptoms. Do you want to sleep until one in the afternoon? Would you prefer employment without extensive human relationships, working by yourself, in almost openly antagonistic monologic-al relation to a hidden crowd of passive, anonymous audience members who never get their say except to applaud you, in a dark, low-ceilinged room whose basic currency is alcohol? In the rest of your life, do you want always to live outside of the mo-ment, crafting cutting observations about existence in its minu-tiae, the basic flaws and weaknesses that make us human beings? Are you looking for a way to heap unforgiving aggression alter-nately onto strangers and yourself? Do you feel so cold, alone and unloved in a godless universe that a basic display of caring decency, such as using the requested term "little person" as op-posed to the hurtful "midget," sends you into an irrational fit of rage? Cool, you're up next.

There is a difference, of course, between being miserable and being depressed. The former is a sensibility; the latter is a med-ical condition. To an extent, I cherish my misery—I come by it honestly, and I'm comfortable with it; I think it makes me funni-er, a bit acidic, and it hasn't stopped me from living my life, par-ticularly with my brilliant and markedly non-miserable wife. Our daughter is an invincibly happy baby, constantly smiling, but if she were to grow up to be a little bit miserable, I could handle that and might even enjoy the opportunity to bond with her in smirking at the giddily, stupidly happy. Contrarily, I'd throw my-self across train tracks to keep her from ever being depressed—as the train is coming by, of course, not just an idle, empty set of train tracks, which would be a depressingly anticlimactic gesture.

That said, it's easy to offer grand sacrifices if you've been feel-ing suicidal. One time, in my early twenties, I confronted a man who was roughing up a woman outside my apartment building in the middle of the night; he told me he had a gun, and she said he probably did, and he kept threatening to pull it out. I've al-ways been proud of myself for staying until she was out of harm's way, but I think, in retrospect, that I have to dock some brav-ery points given this was a time in my life when once or twice I'd played with knives and was indulging in a fair bit of suicidal ideation. Self-sacrifice, in this context, is a bit like offering to pick up somebody's drink when you were planning to go for coffee anyway.

One of the most insidious things about depression is that, like addiction, at its profoundest depths, the very thing you're trying to fight is also your only source of solace. In the midst of depression, every human emotion besides despair rings at a frequency you can't hear—your choices are to feel nothing, a numbness, or else sharp, sobbing pain. You may be surprised to hear that, given these two options, sometimes the nothing feels worse. It's like that episode of *The Simpsons* when the students of Springfield Elementary are stranded on an island and one of the twins, Sherri or Terri, says, "I'm so hungry, I could eat at Arby's." You just want to feel *something* all the way through.

But salvation—and by "salvation" I mean the non-emergency, low-grade ambivalence that most people have as a baseline feeling and take for granted every day—is on the other side of that grey numbness. I've gotten out of depression with pills, and I've gotten out of depression with therapy, talk and slow, deliberate work, and both ways come up through that miserable nothing. When I was trying to do it without pharmaceuticals, I had to set humiliatingly modest goals, then parlay the confidence that I got from accomplishing them into ever-so-slightly-less-humiliatingly-modest ones the next day. Get outside the house at some point today; make it around the block tomorrow. It's painful at first; your eyes haven't seen light in a while. That can trick you into thinking the dark is a more comfortable place to be.

For his analytical and prescriptive book about the Great Recession, *New York Times* columnist Paul Krugman chose the (to me, hilariously) imperative title *End This Depression Now!* Although his book is about the economy, I always giggle at the thought of that title as a screaming injunction from someone who doesn't understand mental illness. Economic depression and personal, emotional depression aren't entirely dissimilar: both are vicious cycles in which catastrophic situations destroy the confidence that things will ever not be catastrophic and, in so doing, make the present situation into an even bigger catastrophe. To get out of either set of circumstances requires outside stimulus to create the conditions in which one can reasonably expect that risking a trepidatious step will bring rewards, rewards that can then be reinvested in the reasonable hope of yet bigger ones. Doesn't "quantitative easing" sound like something a psychologist could also do? What I'm saying is, although they lack the romance of paradox, if you want to understand depression, don't turn to comedians; look to the Keynesian economists.

E for END OF THE WORLD

for End of the World

HUMAN EXISTENCE IS a little bit like *The Godfather Part III*, in that from the very moment it begins, we start to wonder when it's going to end. For all of our history, dark fantasies about the fiery or watery or, later, mushroom-cloudy end of the world as we know it have proven irresistible, so much so that it's tough to find a major civilization anywhere, at any time, that couldn't offer up a fairly spectacular version of how everything will terrifyingly and inevitably grind to a halt. On hearing or reading these old stories, it's almost impossible not to indulge in what historian E.P. Thompson called "the enormous condescension of posterity"; because we're still here to learn about them, by definition these apocalyptic scenarios are silly, so we snicker at them. The past gives us tales of Noah's flood, and we sail away safely on the snark we've built.

Some of us, anyway. Tim LaHaye's Rapture-centred *Left Behind* novels, with their chilling tales of the scramble for survival by those uncalled to join God in Heaven at the End Times, have sold in the millions and achieved, in 2014, the highest honour bestowed by Western society: being made into a Nicolas Cage movie. (It may seem like I'm being hard on the Coppola family in this essay, but that's really not my intention—we're talking about the Apocalypse now.) As predicted in the Book of Revelation, the film received a rating of 2 percent on Rotten Tomatoes, and, perhaps most cruelly, it also starred Lea Thompson. I say cruelly because Thompson, of course, is best known as Lorraine, the matriarch of the *Back to the Future* universe—and whereas *Back to the Future* offered a world wherein human ingenuity, manifested in time travel, might give us the opportunity to fix past mistakes in the hope of a better tomorrow, the Rapture once again reduces us to the status of ineluctably fucked pawns of an unforgiving fate.

There's something wonderfully pathetic—in the sense of being full of pathos, easy to sympathize with—about the ways in which human beings negotiate our irresistible fears of civilizational mortality. I grew up in the 1980s, during the first wave of Pit Bull Panic (our next-door neighbour used to keep a hammer in her baby's stroller for self-defence on walks), and one afternoon, a few of us kids heard that there was a pit bull outside, so immediately we began to work on our defences. We imagined the beast to be such a mighty and merciless hellhound that it couldn't be kept out by my puny ground-level bedroom window. The pane would clearly need fortifications, so we used what we had at hand: my little brother's Mega Bloks. We built a wall of these large light plastic Lego-for-even-smaller-children bricks as reinforcement. If you've never played with Mega Bloks, let me make something clear: it's not possible to build anything with them that couldn't be knocked down by, say, a dying old woman gently tossing the peel of a mandarin orange. This is, in a nutshell, how apocalyptic thinking works in human beings: a desperate, overwhelming and unlikely threat presents itself from out of our imaginations, and then we try to outsmart it in ways that would be humiliatingly puny and ineffective if the threats were in any way real.

A few years ago, I was invited to be the comic relief at an artsy-leftist cultural confab about notions of time and the future—specifically, I was asked to host something called the Populist

Myths of Inevitability Cabaret, in which another comedian and I would riff on a series of internet videos about the end of the world that we had chosen for maximum comedic effect. To get us started, one of the organizers of the conference, Nicholas, sent us a massive dump of links to eschatological videos that he had found online. There were clips about the imminent and alarming extinction of blondes, proof that Prince Charles was the Antichrist, proof that Oprah Winfrey was the Antichrist and, on a cheerier note, a reel of images of floating space-age Polish cities in the year 3050 over a bed of thumping, upbeat techno music.

But the videos that most captured my interest were from the "prepper" subculture—the some-say paranoid, some-say ants-to-our-grasshoppers among us preparing for social breakdown, or what they ominously refer to as "SHTF" situations (for shit hits the fan, the phrase where eschatology meets scatology—though, as Nicholas pointed out, in a shared streak of puritanism none of them ever actually used the swear word). This was *just* before the figure of the prepper entered mainstream culture fulsomely, by way of the main vehicle for introducing North America to its own subcultures: reality TV. In 2012, National Geographic Channel brought *Doomsday Preppers* to air, but this proved to be the high-water mark of a prepper anxiety that, for a few months, seemed weirdly zeitgeisty in the firmament of the Great Recession and white American Obama-hysteria.

In 2009, viewers of the *Today Show* received a peppy introduction to prepper culture in a clip about which there was something almost perfectly American. A smiling multi-ethnic panel of affluent, friendly morning talk show personalities—including weather and weight loss legend Al Roker—unironically throw to a report on a lunatic chiropractor hoarding peanut butter in his basement for when American civilization collapses. It seems the good (almost-)doctor was initially terrified by Y2K, but when that terror failed to materialize he just pulled up his socks like the sectarian follower of some shifty nineteenth-century millennial preacher and got ready for whenever the new date might fall.

The segment's easy back and forth between apocalyptic survivalism and smiley-faced talk show tropes is hilarious: sure, the subtext is the inevitable breakdown of civilization and the descent of the world's first modern democracy and lone superpower into off-the-grid chaos, but that doesn't mean we can't have a little fun from a production standpoint, does it? The man's stocking up on food? Well, then let's score the footage with Duran Duran's "Hungry Like the Wolf." You say he's got "peaches, pancake mix, peas and plenty of peanut butter"? Sounds like it's time for some alliteration! This is what fighting for survival among the ruins of suburban affluence would look like: at one point, we are informed that the family possesses enough water purification tablets to render potable the water in their backyard pool for one year. Is it humanly possible to conjure an image more emblematic of bourgeois paranoia than someone buying water purification tablets for the pool in their own backyard?

As they come out of the piece, the *Today* hosts eat some of the kook's freeze-dried poppyseed cake, with a shelf life of twenty years, complaining that it's dry—then, recovering from this brief moment of pissy incivility, they offer: "But you know what? It has wonderful flavour." America may be ending, but it's still important to be polite when someone gives you a hunk of space-cake.

The most incredible videos we saw, though, were the ones made by the preppers themselves. Unlike the campy, overproduced *Today* segment, these were the low-rent but sincere DIY contributions of preppers doing their best to offer tips to community members preparing for SHTF. There's a gentle and even heartwarming irony to the idea of a congregation of rugged individuals preparing for life off the grid coming together on the internet to help each other out.

One such scrappy entry, uploaded in 2010—the year the Tea Party roared through Obama's first midterm elections—features a gentleman offering a family-friendly recipe for what he referred to, with equal parts whimsy and panic, as "Martial Law Burgers."

There's a lot to love about this video, starting with its opening two-minute-fifty-one-second steady, unbroken shot into a bag of dried adzuki beans, interrupted only occasionally by the man semi-ecstatically running his hands through them. Then there's the prepper's desperate need to telegraph that he is not, whatever it may look like, even though he's teaching you how to make a burger out of adzuki beans, a vegetarian. Throughout the clip, he asserts and desperately reasserts that he is "the furthest thing from a vegetarian that you can possibly imagine": "If there is a point where being a vegetarian begins," he pleads, "I am on the other side of the world." Towards the end of the video, as he looks at his own meatless creations, he says mournfully, "I'd rather it be meat—beef or deer or something." Get it? He loves meat, okay? He's going to teach you how to make a bean-based burger, because when SHTF you're not likely to be able to reliably get your hands on much animal flesh, but he wants—*needs*—you to know that he'd rather it were meat. It's like if the world's biggest homophobe were offering an online tutorial in how to suck cock *just in case it could save your life.*

The best part of the video, though, is the prepper's sunny idea of what civilizational collapse will entail. Judging by the recipe he's sharing, the only thing affected by the Apocalypse will be the availability of beef. Otherwise, from what I can tell, we'll still be able to count on a ready stock of exotic spices like chili and cumin, as well as a steady supply of electricity for our food processors. Processed and cheddar cheeses will be accessible (from milk produced, one has to assume, by fleshless cows), and you'll be able to gorge yourself on that staple of bomb shelter cuisine, "tightly packed fresh cilantro." At one point in the preparation process, as he adds a dollop of salsa to the mix, the chef even implores you to opt for a "smoky salsa," out of the presumably infinite range of salsas you'll have to choose from amid the carnage, wreckage and looting. If this is how it'll be, who can wait for the SHTF (in this case: salsa hits the fajita)?

But how will you pay for your cilantro after the fiat currency collapses along with the government that props it up? Well, by bartering, of course. It's possible that the most heartbreaking video on the internet—and I'm including all the porn—is a prepper clip called "Bartering Material," in which a male narrator shows off the stash of chocolate liqueurs, given to him every Christmas by his father, that he is saving to use as bartering chits for after SHTF. Let's review: every year, this man's father buys him the same terrible gift of waxy chocolate liqueur, and he proceeds to *hoard them as potential currency* for the end of the world (in the meantime, he tells us, he allows himself a single tray to repeatedly bring out for parties). The one redeeming bit of good news here is that, according to him, he has never tried to get drunk on them—then it's right back to tragic when he pronounces Grand Marnier as "Grand Mariner." In another contribution to post-SHTF economics, "Bartering After Collapse," the host-prepper imagines a hypothetical situation in which one might be able to trade silver with someone heading up to Canada to buy medication for his daughter. As we watched the video, Nicholas pointed out that, even in this man's conception of a dissolved, charred and smoking post-American landscape, friendly Canada is just over the still-functional border, and *still* has better, cheaper medicine. There's something super comforting about the permanence that comes with Canadian boringness. You can almost hear the Canadian border guard in this scenario: "Good afternoon, sir. You folks still havin' that nasty lawless descent into a Hobbesian nightmare of all against all? Say, that's a tough bit of business, huh? Oh, well—here are your antibiotics. You take care, eh?'

Of course, SHTF isn't just a masculine affair. In "Baby & Gun," a gorgeous blonde hausfrau instructs viewers in how to properly hold both an infant and a handgun, sharing helpful hints such as using one hand to cover the child's ear while simultaneously pulling the other ear against one's chest, to protect baby's precious little pink eardrums from the barrage of gunfire let loose by the other hand. When I saw it, the top-voted comment underneath this video read: "Beautiful woman, cute kid, great firearm.

What's not to love!" As a lust object for paranoiacs, the "Baby & Gun" tutor is the personification of a backyard pool filled with purification tablets: the intersection of SHTF and MILF. Something about her makeup, the Costco art behind her as well as her violently traditionalist femininity is, I assume, reassuring to the hyper-conservative prepper. Just like the Apocalypse won't stop the flow of delicious cumin, the end of the world doesn't mean that normative gender performance goes out the window: soft-voiced ladies will still look pretty and take care of the babies after the collapse; they'll just have to carry guns, too. "That is it," she says at the end of the video. "We're going to go out shopping now."

As this more-than-slightly-haughty essay shows, even without posterity, it's easy to be condescending. Those of us who don't read Tim LaHaye novels or invest in purification tablets for bodies of water that we own can giggle at the feeble-but-intensive preparations being made against imaginary Armaggedons. Of course, of the incredible achievements of the modern age, not least has been the laying of foundations for what may be humanity's first secular fears of the End. The nuclear age that followed World War II, as well as our entry into what some scientists call the Anthropocene era—the suicidal epoch of man-made climate change—have been times in which several events have revivified our fears that the End is nigh, albeit this time with verifiable data-driven science to back them up: the threat of superpower conflagration, desertification, rising sea levels and the development of a KFC sandwich using hunks of chicken instead of bread. Because human history has been, among other things, an unbroken series of panics over Armaggedons that have failed to materialize, there's a natural giggling skepticism about atomic and climatic Chicken Little-ism. But in the same way that being paranoid doesn't mean they aren't after you, just because you've always worried about something that's never happened doesn't mean it never will. Can I offer a bit of advice? Two words: adzuki beans.

for Fat

"HOW DO WE get liquid fat?" asked the innocent home economics teacher. When I see it happening in my indelible memory of that moment, I want to pounce on her like a secret service agent under a hail of gunfire, trying desperately to prevent catastrophe.

"How do we get liquid fat?" she asked, just a few weeks into grade eight, the very beginning of high school, in homeroom, the very beginning of the day. Each of us was still sizing each other up, sizing ourselves up, breathlessly negotiating a new world so much more sordid than the elementary school we'd left behind just months before. Some students brought clouds of intrigue with them, some fluffy and cumulus, some dark harbingers of storminess: there were kids who had already had sex, apparently, who legend had it had fucked on, or was it underneath, a trampoline. Even this home economics teacher, who was perhaps not as innocent as she'd initially appeared, came with a mythos: she had, supposedly, decades previously, posed for *Playboy*. Whenever anyone had the temerity to doubt the story, the archives of somebody's long-subscribing dad or uncle would be invoked as evidence that it had happened, though somehow the issue—professed to have been seen by so many—was never produced.

Whatever the real story, from the grotto to grade eight home ec she'd journeyed, and now here she was, speaking not like a real teacher, but rather like a teacher in some script for a kids' show, delivering obvious set-up lines, setting up volleyballs of early adolescent trauma for young bullies to spike.

"How do we get liquid fat?"

"Drain Chuck!" said the thin good-looking boy sitting next to me. I crumpled at the retrospective inevitability of his line. I wasn't stunned or surprised—I jumped immediately to resignation (to be describable as "resigned" is a sad enough thing at thirty-five, fifty years old—but thirteen?). Each of us in this new school was being defined and categorized for the length of our stay here, and just like some people were *Playboy*-posers or trampoline-fuckers, I was going to be a giant waddling water balloon filled with liquid fat. *Yup*, I thought, *Drain me. That sounds about right. Now, if you'll excuse me... Are any of these* gas *ovens?*

Later that year, as I was speaking to my friend Helen in the hallway outside English class, an older boy announced loudly in my direction that "Someone in this hallway has tits!" to which charming Helen, in a touching moment of I'm-Spartacus-style solidarity, responded, "Why, thank you!"

In those years of my life, breasts were far more likely to play a defensive than erotic role. To go through high school as a very fat kid is to go about the most sexually terrifying period of one's life from within a carapace of unfuckability. The romantic prospects of a fat guy, such as they are, are summed up in the lyrical image of the leering, corpulent ride attendant who operates Bruce Springsteen's "Tunnel of Love." We are the toothless carnies of the romantic world, lecherous but essentially impotent, occasionally present as comic props when regular people touch each other, but always bound by that most ancient law of Eros: NO FATTIES IN THE TUNNEL.

At the height of the It Gets Better campaign, wherein prominent and successful gay adults shared their stories of hope and overcoming adversity with LGBTQ youth, I was tempted to reach out to chubby youngsters—multi-chinned, breasted boys like I had been—with my own message of It Pretty Much Stays Really Shitty. You will be as welcome on the summery ocean shore as the *Exxon-Valdez*, I would tell them. Your personal style of dress will be dictated almost entirely by who makes an XXL. And fat men don't have it the worst. If our society finds us gross or asexual or laughable, for some sick reason, or reasons, it just flat out hates fat women. In something like a perverse inversion of the gender wage gap, fat men earn only two-thirds of the misery for the same BMI as their female counterparts.

In a sensitive 2010 interview, irreverent comedian Sarah Silverman was asked if anything was "out of bounds" for her comedically, and she explained her refusal to join the psychotic dog pile on fat women, pointing out that popular culture treats them as unworthy of love. She then contrasted this with what was in those *According to Jim* and *King of Queens* dominated days a bona fide cultural phenomenon in stark contrast to my high school experience: sitcoms featuring conventionally flawless women married to men generally shaped like Grimace, the ambiguous purple McDonald's mascot who looked like something suctioned out of a customer's artery.

In my late twenties I was painfully aware of the fat guy/hot wife sitcom trope, because by that time I was living it. More than one friend had pointed it out to me (by the way, guys—thank you *so much* for that). It was a tremendous reversal of romantic fortunes from those of my formative years, and I can't account for it, except to say that I married a Chinese Canadian, so pretty much all white people must have looked at least a *little* fat to her.

When my wife and I got married we didn't get any of the tense, exciting drama that movies and television had led us to believe accompanied the marriage of white dudes and Chinese girls. Her parents weren't worried that I would, say, force her to acknowledge the solar new year. They were cool with a white son-in-law; they were even cool with a white son-in-law who was an aspiring comedian and who planned to subsidize that low-earning passion with something more lucrative ("Don't worry, Mom and Dad—he's also a freelance theatre reviewer!"). They welcomed me into the family with open arms, and the only point of cultural misunderstanding came from the fact that they couldn't quite wrap those arms all the way around me.

See, my in-laws grew up in Hong Kong surrounded by a lot of lean, thin people eating leafy green vegetables; conversely, I grew up around a lot of Pizza Pops. The first time I heard them use the phrase "BBQ pork bun," I thought I'd just been given a cruel nickname. There are, though, many overlapping components to Hong Kongese and fat-guy culture—I felt perfectly at home at my first ten-course banquet, for instance, even if I was used to having all that stuff in a single sandwich.

One arena, however, in which there is absolutely no overlap between Hong Kong and the stretch-marked of the earth is fitting rooms. I don't generally make it a point to highlight physiological differences between ethnic groups—down that road lie the horrors of phrenology, eugenics, Molotov's earlobes being examined before his sit-down with Ribbentrop and amateur comedians' meditations on the size of black phalluses. I *will* say that my friend Nick has a tiny Italian-Canadian father whose biggest claim to fame in the realm of physicality is that when it comes to clothes, he's a "Hong Kong Large." Before my marriage, I had gone through life blissfully unaware of the intricacies of the Hong Kong sizing system, until my in-laws began returning from trips back home with bags full of gifts for their beloved children—of which I was now, terrifyingly, one.

Here in North America, the *X*s on shirt tags are like little kisses that the manufacturer has written into a love note for the chubby shopper: *Mwah! Hope you like the shirt! We love you just the way you are!* Contrarily, tags on clothing from Hong Kong also sometimes have *X*s, but they're more like the strike icons on *Family Feud*—*Bzzt! Wrong Answer! You Will Never Fit This Shirt! Stop Eating So Many Cheezies!*—or pencil marks on an early draft of a guest list, cancelling out an invitation.

Upon returning from their trips back home, Mom and Dad would gather us together, producing a bag of sartorial goodies from the land of cheapest clothes (well, without getting into the labour theory of value, the cheapest hourly rates for *making* clothes); my wife and siblings-in-law would smile, while my heart would drop into my stomach, covering itself in Cheezies dust.

Year after year, we went through the same humiliating dance—my in-laws would smilingly give me a shirt from Hong Kong that I could tell on sight would never fit, because in the United States it would have been sold as a napkin. Upturning my mouth in an excruciating faked smile of my own, I would go into another room, try unsuccessfully to pull it down past my nipples, somehow wrench it off, then return shaking my head.

The whole thing was unpleasant enough on the surface, but on a deeper level, my tight-shirted misery was estranging me from a meaningful family ritual. The bag of presents they would bring home from their trips was my in-laws' way of showing us how much we'd been missed, how much they'd been thinking of us. By including me in their shopping, they were including me in their family. Instead, the opposite feeling would take hold. I'd watch my bodybuilder brother-in-law slip comfortably and effortlessly into whatever he'd been given, and feel not only not part of his family but a member of a different, vastly inferior species altogether. Specifically, one whose evolutionary surroundings hadn't called forth cheekbones.

But maybe It Does Get Better, even for fatties. Things began to shift slightly when my wife's dad returned once from a solo trip, producing another dread bag of presents, casting over me the usual dark cloud—the shadow of which, at least, fit me perfectly. At first, it seemed like more of the same: out of the bag, he produced a bizarre T-shirt with an anthropomorphized hamburger on it, jumping on a trampoline. I still don't know what it means; there was no one making love underneath or on top of it. When he stepped out of the room, I tried desperately to wriggle into it to no avail. What's worse, as in every fat guy's worst nightmare, he walked back in on me while the shirt was only halfway on, exposing my stomach and hourglass figure to the man who helped make my wife. The blood rushed to my cheeks—though not quite enough drained from my torso to make the shirt fit.

You can imagine, then, my terror when he told me it was okay, he had another present. Had I not been debased enough? Did my wife not have a big enough collection of Hong Kongese pyjama shirts? But instead, rather than a tiny sweater, or a button-down that fit me like a miniature vest on an organ grinder's monkey, Dad produced a beautiful wood and leather wristwatch. I was overwhelmed. It was an unexpected gift double-time—a beautiful piece that I would cherish and, at last, an admittance into the homecoming experience.

Later on, I waxed familial for my wife about the experience, mooning over the fact that her family—*my* family—had finally gotten it, finally brought me in. She looked at me with soft eyes and a sweet smile, her warm beautiful face radiating love as she told me that it had been her who'd told him to nix the clothes, just go for a watch. I was deflated—though not literally, sadly. In the end, it turns out we can't be deflated, or drained. I've come to realize that, beyond trying one's best to maintain healthiness with exercise and reasonable vittles, there's nothing useful in dwelling on the negative when it comes to shape, or in beating our ample selves up. Life's too short to spend it hating, or feeling imprisoned within, one's own body. None of us has much time here on earth—and I should know: I've got a watch that, by some miracle, fits around my big fat wrist.

G FOR GOLF

for Golf

THERE ARE MANY activities in life at which one can have a lot of fun without being any good: singing, for instance, or dancing, bowling, being the prime minister of Italy. The joy comes not from success or from executing the task well but from the incidental fun had along the way. I have always been grateful for activities such as these, because by whatever accidents of nature or nurture, I happen to have gone through life with a paucity of ability or skill. I'm not good at things.

Since the beginning, I've been pretty funny; I've generally slotted in at upper-mid-level intelligence; I'm a good public speaker; and I'm excellent with babies and children, but the preceding is a more or less exhaustive list of my talents. In every other field, my tendency is towards failure or incompetence, particularly when it comes to making my body do things that my mind would like it to do. As a child, I played scoreless, non-competitive YMCA basketball (*of course you did,* sighs the reader), and I sunk a total of two shots over the length of my career (and of the two, one of those ought not to count, because I didn't have to make it past any defensive players; I was scoring on my own team's net). I played Little League baseball for several seasons, and I have no recollection whatsoever of ever connecting bat and ball over the plate—though I can *vividly* remember my coach, who was a grown man, desperately making up reasons why I had to stay in the dugout rather than play. In grade eight, the apron I sewed for home economics class looked as though it had been put together by a team of rabid badgers on a work-release program, then torn apart again by an entirely different group of badgers motivated by a deep-seated ideology of hate. My dad used to keep my apron alongside the display-ready, meticulous one made by my brother, I suppose so that he could play games of Guess-Which-One-of-My-Sons-Has-a-Fine-Motor-Skills-Deficiency-and-Which-One-Is-Gay. It was enough of a running gag in my family that my brother wore my apron when he gave the best man toast at my wedding.

For a week or two of one preteen summer, my cousin Steve and I spent a few hours a day at a low-rent pitch and putt golf camp learning, or in my case failing to learn, how to golf. I remember almost nothing of the camp, except that I was briefly infatuated with a girl-golfer my age with whom I shared a few longing glances and zero words; I was equally talented at basketball, baseball, golfing and flirtation—a quadruple non-threat. There were no muscle memories left after golf camp either—no swing, no putt; the lines of communication between my mind and body were still about as effective as a tin can connected by string to a block of cement.

And it's too bad, because if dancing, singing, bowling or being prime minister of Italy are examples of things at which you can stink but still have fun, the game of golf is an almost perfect example of the opposite.

Being so terrible at so many things, for me the feeling of failure is nearly constant, a state of being I don't think I could survive if I weren't able to be stoic or ironic about that failure most of the time. But there's something about golf that is uniquely tantrum-producing. I'm bad at chess, for instance, so when I used to play as a teenager I would make excuses—which, granted, is super annoying—but I don't think I ever played a game of golf growing up during which at some point I didn't cry or yell or somehow act out. I think it has to do with the immutability of golf. With basketball, say, even if I'm useless at scoring, a fat man can still throw a pretty good pick on defence, planting his feet and folding one hand over the opposite wrist with the grace of a nightclub bouncer. Every game of golf I've ever played, though, has begun with the hope that maybe this is the time it all comes together, followed by two or three holes of hopeless incompetence, followed by the sinking realization that I am locked onto the rails for fifteen more holes of exactly the same thing.

Happily, as a grown man, I no longer pitch screaming fits or cry. (Imagine, crying about golf! As an adult, if I'm crying you better believe it's over something important—like a vague sense of dread or a quickly resolved confrontation with a co-worker.) I do still act out, though; at least last time I did. On my most recent golfing excursion, for a bachelor party six years ago, I got so drunk that I stopped to make sand angels in a trap. As embarrassed as I may be by that behaviour now, it was by far the most fun I've ever had on a golf course, replete with consequence-free, fully sauced driving in the cart. As I gassed the little vehicle, swerving with the wild gesticulation of the warmed-over soul, I couldn't believe that just a few decades ago it was socially acceptable to get behind the wheel of a car in the same state.

But, of course, the links are where you go when you want to pretend that the last few decades haven't happened. Whatever the discussions on racial and gender politics unfolding at the golf club, it's safe to assume that they're roughly the same ones that the rest of society was having thirty years ago. If "canaries in the mine shaft" is the go-to metaphor for those affected earliest by social change, then "the boys at the nineteenth hole" could just as effectively signal the contrary. Already known as the sport where rich, powerful white men plot their continued rule of the planet, an exclusive club to which the anti-subalterns have been loath to admit anybody else, even in specific cases the forces of golf tend to be on the wrong side of history. Superstar

Tiger Woods has been subject to not one but *two* artless, un-funny fried chicken jokes from fellow high-level players: one from Sergio Garcia, the other from something called a Fuzzy Zoeller, which I'm informed is a man and not a horrible eu-phemism. American tycoon/pustule Donald Trump famously went to war with a Scottish community to build a resort that ex-perts feared would ruin coastal dunes, then got mad when the Scots wanted to build a wind farm next to it (generally speaking, if even Scottish people don't want your golf resort, you've gone too far; a Scot complaining about the presence of golf is rough-ly equivalent, in the vernacular of ethnic stereotyping, to a pan-icked German yelling, "Shut it down! Zis factory is vay too ef-ficient!"). Golfer Phil Mickelson briefly became the poster boy for mewling crybaby neoliberal tax reform when he threatened to leave California to escape the state's confiscatory taxes on his winnings (he should pick grapes without documentation in-stead—California doesn't take *any* taxes from those guys). And, of course, the proximate cause for the early 1990s confrontation between Mohawk warriors and Canadian and Québécois po-lice and armed forces at Oka was the proposed expansion of a nine-hole course to eighteen, which gives you a pretty good idea of whose comfort and profit the violence of the colonial-settler state is really *fore!*

All of this social backwardness is useful for me to keep in mind. In recent years I have soothed my chronic failure at golf with self-congratulating distance. Like a righteous man who refuses to eat foie gras that he can't afford anyway, I have re-nounced the game of golf for its racism and sexism, its class ex-clusion, its overuse of water resources and pesticides, its unwill-ingness to pay taxes or accommodate its neighbours. Golf is a social evil, for all these reasons. Any seething, unresolved feel-ings of lifelong personal failure are purely coincidental.

for HETERONORMATIVITY

for Heteronormativity

WHEN I WAS about twenty years old, my brother around seventeen, our dad took us out for what was meant to be a nice family dinner at one of Vancouver's tackiest sushi restaurants. Fairly close to a university, the place's tagline was "Miso Horny" (Get it? Just like that war zone Asian sex worker in that movie!), and it was done up in quasi-Tiki decor that seemed designed to reassure frat boys in their choice of shell necklace. Ringing the outside of the dining area were normal tables, but up the middle were a collection of semi-enclosed, ersatz–South Pacific hut-tables, one of which had been reserved by my dad.

There was, however, a hitch in the plan (one that went beyond mere matters of good taste). For whatever reason, the diners that night were taking an inordinately long time in the Tiki huts. Dad was uncharacteristically ornery and short-tempered about the seating arrangements, insisting that he had reserved a hut for his family. For our parts, my brother and I—being, with the exception of a few forever-lagging body parts, grown men—squinted in petulant confusion: *Who the fuck cares?* Insisting that we were hungry and largely uninterested in themed seating, we cajoled Dad into accepting the host's offer of a regular table along the wall. Once seated, Dad nervously and enviously eyed the shelter of the Tiki huts.

As it happens, he hadn't chosen the special tables for the whimsy. He had wanted the privacy of those obnoxious enclosures because he had something important to tell us. But having screwed up his courage for the big night, he wasn't going to stop now.

"I'm gay," he said.

We sat quietly for a second, absorbing his words, reading his sweet and vulnerable and expectant face.

"Is that why the house is always so clean?" I asked.

The revelation was sort of a non-surprise surprise. This was just a few months after my little brother had come out of the closet, so it felt like a time in my life when if somebody had something important to tell you, it was probably that they were gay. Our family was like something produced by the writers' room on a stale sitcom, turning everybody gay as a means of producing a host of zany new plot lines.

But my brother's coming out had been a mere formality—as a kid playing dress-up, Nick had cycled through more princesses than the British paparazzi. He took a minute out of his schedule, the tiny open space between giving shoulder rubs and making collages out of celebrity magazines, to tell the folks closest to him that he was gay. He didn't even bother to tell my aunts and uncles; he just started showing up at family gatherings with dudes and nobody batted an eye. Things were different with my dad; I'd always thought he had a moustache because he was French.

I'd known that Dad embodied a different kind of masculinity. It was one that I revelled in and sought to pattern my own after (See? How butch is it to get excited about patterns?). He was handsome, strong, clean and well dressed; he took us to the symphony, to see Shakespeare; he knew nothing about sports or cars and, just as importantly, was totally unperturbed by his lack of knowledge. He was the kind of man I wanted to be—we could love live theatre *and* breasts! As a young kid, I'd felt a trill of superiority over the idiot boys who played soccer on the gravel field at recess and lunch while my friend Chad and I went off to a remote corner of the playground where two of our female classmates would lie down on top of us (though a word to the wise: don't do this if you have a younger brother who gets out of kindergarten at lunch hour and your Mom waits for him at a car that's parked where she can clearly see your little junior swingers excursion).

The guys-'n'-sports-sports-'n'-guys incarnation of masculinity always seemed to be a world full of homosocial platitudes, plus a lot of running and sweating. Who gave a shit about sports? Better to be a man like my dad. When the Vancouver Canucks made their run to the Stanley Cup finals when I was thirteen, I pretended to care because my high school crush, Kathleen, would hold my hand as we watched the game at a birthday party and squeeze when the Canucks did something exciting (having been taught nothing about the game by my father, I had no other metric for assessing what was going on).

Not that I wasn't occasionally tempted by the musky side of masculine gender "performance"—Judith Butler's term was an apt descriptor of my theatrical attempts at butch. Succumbing to peer pressure and wanting, Pinocchio-like, to be a real boy, I bought a car magazine one day, memorized a handful of incomprehensible (to me) statistics about the engines and then, having no means of contextualizing them on my own, took wild guesses as to which were impressive. I practised speaking about them in excited—no, rapturous—tones, assigning random emphases to various terms and syllables.

I remained, though, largely mystified by straight male culture. When we were sixteen years old, my friends and I, all young communists, pined to visit Castro's Cigar Lounge downtown— without fake IDs, though, it seemed as much a long shot as when a band of rebels disembarked the good ship *Granma* only to face the troops of Fulgencio Batista (incidentally, I have no recollection of what we expected to find in Castro's Cigar Lounge— doubtless some Marxist salon with overstuffed leather chairs and a libertarian approach to smoking bylaws). One night, unable any longer to resist our curiosity, we did our best to age-up, carefully choosing our clothes and sneaking into my friend's older brother's room for some hair gel, because for reasons I can't possibly understand today, we apparently didn't have access to our own hair gel. Crossing the threshold into Castro's, passing a collection of billiard tables, we moved to the bar and asked for the pool balls, which were handed to us without a fuss. We'd done it; exchanging sly smiles, we made our way to the felts. On the way, I noticed an attractive server dressed in tiny aggressively sexual cut-offs. In a fit of extraterrestrial naïveté, I (honestly) thought to myself: "Those are inappropriate—it's weird that her boss lets her wear those to work." We then noticed on the wall a tacky pastel line drawing of a naked woman with feathered hair—the kind of thing a young man in the early 1980s might have dreamed of airbrushing onto the side of a van. Just as we began piecing together where we were, a stage in the far corner of the room began to fill with artificial fog. Our feminist sensibilities outraged (yes, really), the four of us hightailed it, beating a tactical retreat in tribute to the guerrillas before us. (In the years since, sitting in the sad sobriety of post-ejaculation, closing the browser window, I've often wondered where that sweet sense of shock went.)

In truth, much as I'd patterned my own heterosexuality after my father's heterodox approach, I remembered, in the aftermath of his announcement, that I'd suspected he might be gay back when I was thirteen. It was a few years after my mother had died and Dad was seeing a lot of his friend Don—a sweet doe-eyed man with whom he would sit in his room with the door closed and watch movies (Jesus Christ, was I ever so fucking gullible? I feel like even a six-year-old waiting for the Easter Bunny to arrive would have nudged me and said, "Hey, get a load of the queers!"). Lying in bed beneath a Montreal Canadiens pennant that signified 100-percent ethnic affiliation and 0-percent interest in actual sports, I would pray to God that neither my dad nor I was gay. I'm not totally sure where that came from—it wasn't what I'd been raised with. I think it just seemed, to me, like a burdensome, shitty thing to have to deal with; in which case, I don't think I was incorrect. That said, there was clearly some adolescent homophobia (in this case literally fear, terror) in the mix.

Responding to a behaviour problem reported by my teachers and school administrators, my dad had threatened to enroll me in a local private all-boys school, a fate made scarier to me by the academy's colloquial name, Homo High; Dylan, one of the other class clowns/denizens of the principal's office, would taunt me that I was going to be sent to Gaylesbian School, running the words together into his own little portmanthomo. If only I'd known to call my single dad's bluff: there was no way he could have afforded to send me to private school.

In the instant my dad came out of the closet, the only thing that worried me was what it might mean about my parents' relationship. To have a sham marriage added to my dead mother's collection of tragedies would have been far too much to handle—I'd sooner have spent a thousand summers at Gaylesbian School. Dad calmly assured us that he and Mom had loved each other very much, that it was a real marriage and that if she were still alive, they'd still be together. I believed him, which, at the time, may have been another case of Watching-Movies-with-Don gullibility. But later on, my dad's mom put my mind at ease. She told me about Dad's first coming out, when he was about twenty, after he'd left Montreal and arrived on the West Coast, sending a letter home to his mother explaining to her what she already knew: that for her *petit chou, hommes* was where the heart is. She had written back with her unconditional love and support, explaining— as I understand that many mothers do—that she'd always known. Some time later, he wrote to tell her he was in love with a woman, and she told him he didn't have to pretend. He assured her that he wasn't pretending, that he was in love, with a woman—my mother—and they were getting married. The whole story sounds even sweeter in French. My panic about the authenticity of my parents' romance was satisfactorily dismissed.

What I probably should have been worrying about, instead, was losing my model of a cool, gentle, sophisticated hetero-sexual manhood. As the sole familial responsibility for vaginal intercourse fell on my shoulders, I was left behind. I'd grown up thinking that the men in my family were swans, more elegant and sophisticated than the ugly ducklings surrounding us. As it turned out, though, that was only partially right—Dad and my brother were swans, but I was just a duck, and, in the end, as they opened their white wings to their full breadth to take flight, I'd have to learn to live among my own kind, sinking into mel-ancholy as I realized all the other ducks wanted to do was talk about how Anaheim is doing in the NHL Western Conference.

for IMPERIALISM

for Imperialism

As the opening ceremonies of the London Olympics unfolded in the summer of 2012, Piers Morgan—the former right-wing press man turned meanie British reality TV judge turned expat infotainment broadcaster—found it difficult to contain himself. "With the greatest respect to China," he tweeted, referring to the hosts of the previous Summer Games, "don't think they have quite our musical back catalogue as a nation."

In fairness, it's pretty hard to compare the Beatles, the Rolling Stones, Pink Floyd, and The Who to the zero Chinese musicians Piers Morgan has ever listened to. I'm guessing he's heard a few gongs, maybe that faux-Confucian song white kids play at the high end of a piano and a CD of tinkling Buddhist meditation soundtracks and thought to himself, "Well, this isn't as good as Eric Clapton." I don't mean to suggest that Morgan is culturally insensitive. He once wrote a touching piece for the *Daily Mail* online in which he lamented the number of times (500,000) that the n-word appears every day on Twitter, helpfully pointing out that "by comparison, the words 'bro' and 'dude' are only used 300,000 and 200,000 times per day." I am saying that in his electrified response to the opening ceremonies, he may have lapsed into ethnic solipsism. This may explain another of the giddy posts that he ejaculated onto social media during the festivities: "We need to be an Empire again— seriously. #ProudOfBritain."

All in all, it's a strange response to a show that one happens to be enjoying: *These opening ceremonies are so good, they make me feel like reintroducing a formal system of racialized theft of land and resources, de jure or de facto enslavement and brutal hierarchies of immiseration! I mean, I don't understand how anybody could watch this dance number and not immediately follow it up by forcing some Egyptians to dig a canal.*

Imperialism, the idea that white men should be in charge of everything that's going on everywhere, for everybody's sake, is an idea that has proven perhaps unsurprisingly resilient among white men, even putative anti-imperialists. On the fiftieth anniversary of Indian independence, Christopher Hitchens highlighted the underlying absurdity of the Raj in the pages of *Vanity Fair* (a magazine that takes its name from the title of Thackeray's satire of imperial Britain): "As recently as a century ago, the destinies of the world's two most populous civilizations—India and China— were largely in the hands of pink-faced men from a small, rain-sodden, but somewhat talented archipelago in the North Sea." Nevertheless, within six years Hitchens was championing British (and, more importantly, American) sovereignty over Iraq, hyping an invasion so catastrophic that many of his "pink-faced men" were forced to blush an even deeper shade of rose.

One of Hitchens's most outspoken comrades in making the case for the Iraq War was public intellectual and occasional Canadian Michael Ignatieff, who also happens to be a scion of imperial Russia. Over the course of a brief vacation to Toronto and Ottawa a few years ago, Ignatieff attempted to become the prime minister of Canada but found that, among other things, his throaty support for the 2003 invasion of Iraq was a political liability (especially in Quebec, long the seat of Canadian anti-imperialism largely because of an immunity to the charms of Olde England and its majesty). Iggy and his team did their best to play it all down as a mistake, but his contrition was about as convincing as Jackson Pollock apologizing for making that one painting so splattery. Ignatieff's support for the war was not just of a piece with his politics, it was essential to them. Iggy had long been making the argument for a sort of benign, benevolent, postmodern imperialism, a trickle-down, supply-side foreign policy in which the pursuit of American self-interest would help bring the dazed swarthy subalterns of various conflict zones into the warm light of liberal humanist capitalism. He made the case most explicitly in a slight 2003 book called *Empire Lite*—a title that I'm willing to bet he thought was pretty goddamn cute and pretty goddamn clever but still isn't as honest as, say, *The Lite Man's Burden*.

In Ignatieff's world view, Canada, too, was provincial—which is probably why he spent his adult life in Britain and the United States, the hearts of the old empire and the new one. The Conservative Party "attack machine" was widely denounced for characterizing him as "just visiting," but if the criticism stuck it's only because it was so obviously, embarrassingly true. In response, Ignatieff rushed out a book, *True Patriot Love*, about the thoroughbred Canadian pedigree of his maternal family (apparently unaware there's nothing less Canadian than having been in this country for a long time). The loose narrative framework of the piece is his great-grandfather's surveying mission across the country to help plan the railway that would be its spine. So even when he's not trying to be an imperialist, Ignatieff's concept of home involves map-making white men setting out to exercise control over land that doesn't belong to them.

Mr. Ignatieff lost his bid to be prime minister, as we know, to another ecstatic monger of the war in Iraq, Stephen Harper, whose great regret was that Canada wasn't one of the belligerents and whose several renditions of Beatles songs over the years have assaulted the integrity of Piers Morgan's beloved national back catalogue. Prime Minister Harper caused a wave of bemused and angry puzzlement when he said, in 2009, "Canada has no history of colonialism"—a statement roughly equivalent to "this omelette has no history of egg." It was pretty clear that when Harper said "colonialism," he meant imperialism, empire, and in fact an explatory statement from his office alluded to this. Even still, it's an odd thing to say—instead of "this omelette has no history of egg," more like "this egg has no history of chicken."

Although it's true that Canada's ability to project its power offshore falls well short of empire, our whole country is, to put it something less than patriotically, an excrescence of it (for the record, I mean that in the kindest way and I love it here). I live 7,500 kilometres away from London, in a province named British Columbia, in a city named after a captain in the British navy. We hosted the Games once, too, incidentally (and we had the incredible k.d. lang singing Leonard Cohen at our opening ceremonies, if you want to talk back catalogue), and one of the slogans of those, like me, opposed to doing so was "No Olympics on Stolen Native Land." I still think that's a way better slogan than #ProudOfBritain.

for Junk Food

WHEN WE BECAME PARENTS, my wife, Cara, and I assumed the responsibility of codifying values that had until then gone unspoken, developing household policies with regard to Bad Things like drugs; movies with violence, swearing and princess imagery; and junk food. We'll enforce these guidelines with various degrees of strictness and consistency, aware that the moment our daughter leaves our home, even if only for a few minutes, she'll escape our sovereignty and the rules will dissolve as quickly as a sugar cube in the mouth of a wild-eyed child (most likely, her sugar cube and her wild eyes).

We were both raised by parents who'd tried, however quixotically, to enforce unswerving limitations on junk food. The result is that, all these years later, I tend towards being the healthiest-eating fat guy you're ever going to meet. Around the world, but particularly across North America—or, as it's known globally, the "Not That Into Belts" Belt—panic has set in about the damage being wrought by cheap, highly processed junk foods, and whenever the news runs a story contributing to this panic, they use footage of bodies exactly like mine waddling through public spaces without heads. But although I share the stretch marks and self-hatred of the junk food eaters, I don't have their nacho-cheese orange fingertips; for the most part, I'm a binge guy, not a junk guy. Although occasionally even the spelt-breadiest of us goes for something in a bright crinkly bag.

Similarly, my own childhood was not junk food free. Most of my early memories of eating delicious garbage are bound up with my best childhood friend and next-door neighbour, Shaun Zavarise. Shaun and I were both chubby boys and loved each other with the ardour that only children who happen to live close to each other are capable of mustering. To put our platonic infatuation in perspective: one summer evening, a section of the fence separating our backyards collapsed, and Shaun and I marked the occasion by running for hours in a loop between the two properties, celebrating—like Berliners drunk on Pilsner and the collapse of Stalinism—the fact that we were no longer divided. This is why I've always believed that, although good fences make good neigbours, terrible fences make for fucking fantastic ones.

As per Italian-Canadian custom, Shaun's family had a vegetable garden in the backyard, where they grew cherry tomatoes and other earthy goods, but we never ate those. The cherry tomatoes weren't there to be eaten. They were there to be picked by Shaun and hucked at trucks that happened to be driving down our alley, while I cowered in fear at a safe distance. Instead, at Shaun's we treated our toe-dragging metabolisms to quick spikes of all things unwholesome: we ate bag after non-biodegradable, grey bag of bulk nacho chips; one afternoon, we found and drank an entire flat of pop bottles behind the bar downstairs.

Scarface-like, we even got high on our own supply: one afternoon Shaun, my little brother and I decided to open a "store" on the sidewalk in front of our house, setting up an old TV tray, covering it with bags of chips and candy, ready to do business until some older boys came by on their bikes, one of them oozing malice and sunscreen.

"Well, well, well," he said, sounding like Mean Kid #1 in an '80s movie, setting up the protagonist for a sweet revenge to which we in the audience could thrill vicariously. "Selling without a licence? I guess I'll have to confiscate your merchandise." (These were his actual exact words. It seems so bizarrely Canadian, in retrospect, for this young tough to have bullied us using the language of a low-level government bureaucrat.) The kid began to scoop our goods into his arms, until Shaun, who was gigantic, socked him. Wanting to do my part, I went over to the bully's friend—who was sitting on his bike, observing from a polite distance—and shoved him off it. Thusly thwarted, the two older boys rode off down the street, leaving Shaun and me to survey our wares, shrug and decide that the shopkeeper life wasn't for us, before taking the inventory into the backyard to gorge on it.

At our house, junk food, pop and candy were supposed to be for special occasions, but evading this prohibition was as simple as hopping the border to the Zavarises; it drove my parents bananas (another food we never ate next door). Mom and Dad were livid when one night, around midnight, in the middle of a sleepover, Shaun's dad took us to 7-Eleven, a trip they worried might imperil not only my nutritional health but also, in the event of a hold-up, my physical safety. Stories like this—middle-of-the-night trips to 7-Eleven, coupled with the paranoiac fear of an armed robbery—go a long way towards explaining why, today, I am both fat and have to take anti-anxiety medication.

If the bad influence, junk food–wise, was for the most part unidirectional—if my parents were largely blameless in ensuring that when we played G.I. Joe, the initials stood for "glycemic index"—there was one exception, one mouthwatering piece-of-shit food that my parents sent Shaun home with a taste for.

One anomalously junk-leaning meal in rotation at our house was Alpha-Getti on toast—Alpha-Getti being a canned alphabet-shaped pasta that erased any good it might do in the literacy department with its copious amounts of sodium and simple carbohydrates. If you're wondering why we were served pasta on top of bread, it's because my father was always worried that we kids weren't getting enough gluten.

He whipped up a batch of this delicacy one afternoon when Shaun was over to play. Dad followed the family recipe: opened the can of Alpha-Getti; heated it over medium, stirring occasionally; dropped several pieces of bread into the toaster; lacquered them with margarine when they popped back up; covered them with Alpha-Getti; and sprinkled it all with a touch of Kraft "parmesan cheese." He ferried the plates to the table. Shaun took a bite.

Shaun's face lit with a fireworks display of sensual delight. What is this ambrosia, he seemed to be asking of the universe, carried off on a warm bed of pleasure. It truly became Alpha-Getti for him, in the sense that all other pastas would be beta-gettis and gamma-gettis now. He headed home, demanding that Alpha-Getti be added to the regular grocery rotation. The answer—easily spellable with the very treat he was requesting—was no.

Shaun was half-Irish, half-Italian, but in the same way as Henry Hill, Ray Liotta's character in *Goodfellas*: he was Irish enough that he could never be a made guy, but he was Italian in any sense that mattered (Shaun's tiny strawberry-haired mother, Gail, would stand at the stove frying such less-than-Gaelic classics as onions, peppers and sweet sausage). His father, Danny, was an East Vancouver Italian, whose parents had made the long journey from Italy to Nanaimo Street (not a long distance culturally, but in kilometres? Oof, *Marone!*). Although Alpha-Getti dealt in the Roman alphabet, it was insufficiently authentic to pass muster in the Zavarise household. No way was Danny going to welcome into his home this industrial monstrosity, this excremental canned slur against the proud culinary history of a great Mediterranean civilization. Yet, in the end, what could he do? His son was in love.

As in many seemingly intractable cases, the solution was to be found in compromise: Alpha-Getti would be allowed in the house, but on condition that it only be served on toast.

The wisdom and simplicity of that decision remain inspirational to me, and as a father myself now, I hope to try to remain conscious of the main parenting lesson to be drawn from it: so many of the challenges we will face are matters that can be solved with a simple act of reframing, recontextualization. Because as pasta, Alpha-Getti is refuse, an unwholesome and insulting mass market derivative of a great traditional foodstuff. But as a condiment? It can't be beat.

FOR
KELSEY GRAMMER

for Kelsey Grammer

OKAY, NOT REALLY, but we need a *K* entry and, as it turns out, there are not only relatively few things that begin with *K* but they are also disproportionately wonderful: koala bears, kangaroos, the *Kama Sutra*. It takes three *K*s in combination to produce anything truly odious; even the Klingons were rehabilitated as a martial space-race by the time a second generation of *Star Trek* shot out of the cosmos.

There are those who, in my shoes, would have opted for Kardashian—but I find the trend of Kim-bashing to be more baffling than anything else. The chief complaint levelled against her, from what I can tell, is the objection that "she's only famous because she's rich, sexed-up and famous." Yes. In case you hadn't noticed, that's why about 90 percent of the people who are famous are famous. Kim Kardashian is the wealthy, superlatively attractive daughter of a man who acted as defence counsel in the most sensationalized celebrity murder trial in history—in what universe was she not going to be famous if she wanted to be? Glenn Beck is famous and he doesn't even have cheekbones, let alone exquisite ones. Get mad about that.

So, the entry for *K* will be Kelsey Grammer, which I'm sad to report, because I pretty much love him. Grammer has the best voice anybody's had since Paul Robeson (though Robeson's shade of red was communist, whereas Grammer's is Republican; more on that later) and an almost perfectly calibrated sense of comic cornball that goes big and broad without spilling over into too much. He was pitch perfect on *Cheers* and transcendent on *The Simpsons* as the elitist recidivist Sideshow Bob, but it was as the leading man on his own show that Grammer hit me in a deeper place.

For a few years in my twenties, my brother, my father and I were each living in separate cities, and during this time I was drawn to the inseparable-father-and-two-brothers dynamic on display on *Frasier*. One might assume that because both my brother and father are gay, I would have related to the butch, flannel-wearing Martin Crane role, in opposition to the effete aesthetes, Frasier and Niles. But that's not the case. My dad once kindly assured me that I was "the biggest fag in the family," and I've always taken that as a compliment.

But surrogate TV family wasn't the only reason to watch *Frasier*, the last great conventional two-act network sitcom. (The postmodern revolution in the form kicked off by Garry Shandling's twin triumphs, *It's Garry Shandling's Show* and *The Larry Sanders Show*, meant sitcoms would increasingly become self-conscious in their showiness, culminating in mockumentary-style, direct-to-camera addresses, even on shows where that conceit makes no sense. *Frasier* was the last really good sitcom to play it straight.) It was well written and well acted, and it was also a beautiful show, with sumptuous and immaculately designed sets and costumes that framed a lifestyle I coveted. This may be surprising, given my values, but I've never been one of those Marxist ascetics—for me, "champagne socialist" isn't a derogation; it's a life goal. All I've ever asked of fate is to one day be rich enough that my commie politics could be denounced as hypocritical.

That sort of incongruity between identity and ideology is, emphatically, not a problem faced by Kelsey Grammer. Mr.

Grammer is a wealthy white man who possesses the politics of a wealthy white man. That is not to say that he has led a cushiony country-club life; the cumulative details of his tragic biography would make a Patsy Cline album sound like a Tony Robbins seminar. But despite, or because of, these hardships, Grammer is a fairly hard right Republican libertarian (though apparently not libertarian enough to have stopped him from endorsing the wild-eyed theocracy of lunatic presidential candidate Michele Bachmann). In 2010, Grammer backed a fledgling right-wing media venture called RightNetwork—"All that's right with the world"—and made a promotional video in which he listed "big government," "more taxes" and "grown-men tickle-fights" as "things that just aren't right." He once told Jay Leno that he'd been denied an Emmy nomination because he was an "out of the closet Republican"—a comment of triple-crown unpleasantness for including right-wing politics, a self-pitying analogy to a group persecuted by Republicans, and Jay Leno.

I can't remember when, exactly, I learned that Grammer was one of the standard-bearers for Hollywood conservatism. I just remember wishing, when I did, that I hadn't.

The worst part is that I know this response makes me no better than the guy with the Confederate flag truck decals burning his old Dixie Chicks albums (I mean, I guess I'm slightly better than that guy because I don't have Confederate flag truck decals, and I'm not burning any CDs, which can't be good for the environment—but otherwise...). This is a point upon which we human beings are almost universally hypocritical: when artists and celebrities whom we like espouse the same politics as we do, there's almost nothing better—we can't wait to hear them declaim our shared values from behind the podium at an awards ceremony or see them wriggled into a T-shirt, all sinew and silicone, bearing our movement's slogan across their chests. Conversely, when they align themselves with a cause we oppose, we question their right to say anything at all. "What the fuck does Neil Young know about the tar sands? He should just stick to playing the guitar! Now if you'll excuse me, I'm off to a foreign policy symposium with Toby Keith."

The problem, then, isn't Kelsey Grammer but my own un-reasonable desire that, if he doesn't share my view of the world, he restrict his public pronouncements to the subjects of tossed salads and scrambled eggs. If I can't just enjoy watching his show while he leads a full, well-rounded life—which can, and in fact ought to, include political expression—then that's my problem, not his.

Still: in an interview with CNN, Grammer was once asked if he thought his ex-wife, Camille, had married him because he was "Kelsey Grammer, TV icon." He answered, "No—I think she married me because I was Frasier." Camille, I can totally relate.

(Mr. Grammer, if you're reading this: I apologize. I really just needed a *K*. And I'm sorry for streaming *Boss* from a pirate site.)

for Liberals

OF THE MANY challenges and disadvantages that come with living next to the greatest military, economic and cultural superpower in world history, one of the most irritating is the effect on language. I'm not talking about the panic over "Mum" versus "Mom" (like "colour" and "labour," I've always felt that if we want to make a big show of being Canadians, we ought to be spelling it "Moum") but rather those moments when, through its sheer size or gravitational pull, the USA diminishes the specificity of Canadian English. This can happen by its gobbling up a word for its exclusive use, like "America" or "American," for instance— leaving the rest of us who call these two continents home without an easily accessible term to describe ourselves. The American monopoly of this powerful adjective-noun combination is as arrogant as if one day the Germans decided "European" now meant just them, and when people used the term "Europe," what they meant was Germany—which we all know is only true in an economic sense.

But it's not enough for the Americans to take words we need; sometimes, it's a problem of the domestic market being flooded by imports, wherein the specifically Canadian meaning of a word or phrase is washed out by the power of American books, magazines, movies, music and television and replaced with a new significance from south of the border. The term "neo-conservative," for instance, used to mean a whole different thing up here than it did in the States, same with "Céline Dion." Eventually, though, the passive, polite local meaning gets elbowed out of the way by its brash Yankee counterpart, or, in the best-case scenario, the two versions of a word live uncomfortably and inconsistently side by side. As with the word "liberal."

In most of the world, liberalism is seen as a Western European political philosophy rooted in the Enlightenment and situated in the centre of the political spectrum. In the USA, it signifies the raving out-of-control extreme end of the corduroyed left (with apologies to all the amazing but statistically insignificant socialists in the USA). The difference has partly to do with local jargon; basic twentieth-century state interventions that, in the rest of the world, were qualified as "social-democratic" or even "socialist" were, in the USA, called "liberal." But it also has to do with the fact that, politically, the U.S. is like a yin-yang that's white on one side, white on the other; for the past several decades, the lopped-off spectrum of mainstream American politics has run from centre-right to extreme-right, so liberals seem like radicals, however much they may rush to point out that they aren't (as when liberal MSNBC host Rachel Maddow suggested that, added up, the particulars of her world view basically made her an Eisenhower Republican. It's difficult to imagine a figure of the Canadian left making a similar pronouncement—say, Judy Rebick describing herself as a Diefenbaker Tory. That said, even as a leftist I can admit that it would be nice if our present crop of Tories identified more as Diefenbaker Conservatives rather than inclining towards being Louis XIV Conservatives).

Because of the American uses of the word, I have, many times, been described by well-meaning friends lacking in political sophistication as a "liberal." I am not. I am a socialist. Although these world views share certain philosophical wellsprings, we've sorta been doing our own thing for a few centuries now. It's something like calling a radical Anabaptist a Catholic, or referring to *Cheers* and *Frasier* as the same show. It's especially galling for a Canadian radical to be called "liberal" because the centrist big-business party that has governed the country more than any other in our history is, of course, the Liberal Party. In some ways, though, the party has taken advantage of the ambiguity around their name, campaigning as liberals in the American sense, governing as liberals in the European one.

To be fair, over the past few decades the whole Western world has become a leftless, all-white yin-yang, and perhaps it's not just stateside where respectable political conversation doesn't really begin until you've passed over the socialists to get to the centre. That's certainly how many Canadian liberals and Liberals whom I've met would see it. For the past several decades, we socialists have been denied a seat at the grown-ups' table of politics, and while we've been eating chicken fingers off the kids' menu, drawing manifestos and post-structuralist critiques in crayon on the backs of our placemats, liberals have been sitting across from conservatives, honing ever more sophisticated palettes, making tough choices and serious faces.

The older liberals among them can foggily remember when they might have taken a bona fide leftist quasi-seriously—gone and seen a play by Brecht, maybe, or watched *Spartacus.* But the younger ones have only seen *Gladiator.* For these young men in checked shirts with clean haircuts and eyeglasses of tamed funkiness, young women with shining skin and a serenity imparted by yoga and an abiding faith in market mechanisms, the watchword is "pragmatism." These are people who own *The Wire* on Blu-ray and use terms like "muscular" when talking about foreign policy. In their eyes, irrelevance is the greatest possible political crime, and to them, we on the left have embraced it completely, an allegation that I resent. We didn't *embrace* irrelevance, it was *thrust upon us,* so we made ourselves *comfortable;* there's a difference. The biggest insult that can be levelled at the left from the liberal centre is that of "complaining from the sidelines."

While the left whines, the thinking goes, liberals and Liberals are too busy legislating for universal health care, pay equity and marriage equality and against climate change to bother listening.

Of course, liberals gloating to leftists about health care, pay equity, gay marriage or a fighting chance against climate change is a bit like Elvis Presley telling Chuck Berry to thank him for rock 'n' roll. If socialism and liberalism are distinct strands of Enlightenment humanism, then socialists are the hipsters of that humanism, advocating on particular issues before they're cool (also, like hipsters, socialists tend to have horrible beards). Today's easy liberal consensus—gender equality, racial equality, the idea that peg-legged tubercular five-year-olds should get statutory holidays from their coal-sorting jobs—is almost always yesterday's fiery and decidedly un-pragmatic socialist whinge. As it turns out, the middle of the political spectrum is a far more fun, sophisticated place to be after your comrades have already expended a lot of blood, sweat and tears yanking it in the proper direction for you (and guess which direction that usually is?). This is the thing that centrists hate to admit: the moments they're proudest of being liberals is when they're strutting around in our old clothes. Being socialists, though, we don't mind so much sharing credit.

M for MOTHERLESSNESS

for Motherlessness

LONG BEFORE THE ADVENT of *Glee* and the revenge of the nerds, I attended an outlier high school where cool, popular kids were on the debate team and sang in the choir. This may sound like a rationalization from someone who was on the debate team and sang in the choir, but I'm confident that a study of my old yearbooks will bear out my thesis. Choir solos were sought by slick-haired non-virgins as well as the rest of us. The fiercest competition that I can remember was for a moment alone in the spotlight during our junior high rendition of the old African-American slave spiritual "Sometimes I Feel Like a Motherless Child," whose cheerful lyrics run like this:

> Sometimes I feel like a motherless child
> Sometimes I feel like a motherless child
> Sometimes I feel like a motherless child
> A long way from home
> A long way from home

The jostling for this position being as cutthroat as it was, we threw ourselves into practice, trying to put our own fingerprints on the uncomplicated dirge-like melody and straightforward libretto. The simplicity of the song was such that at least one student's mother, overhearing her daughter rehearsing at the piano at home, was convinced that she was making it up herself, on the spot, and began weeping in the next room, no doubt wondering how it was that she had failed her little girl. There are countless versions of the song that any of us could have mimicked, the definitive one belonging to Paul Robeson. Bob Marley sang an iteration, too, called "Where Is My Mother?"—albeit a derivation with a more lawyerly respect for technicality—clarifying that he is not actually motherless, just feels motherless. There is also a lunatic psychedelic jazz interpretation of the original song, recorded in 1970 by Kathleen Emery, whose whole tenor is so wildly inappropriate and contrapuntal that it verges on the transcendent.

But this was the middle 1990s, heyday of the now-forgotten cultural phenomena of "hidden" CD tracks and Hootie & the Blowfish, and "Sometimes I Feel Like a Motherless Child" lies squarely in the middle of a Venn diagram of both. On their 1994 album *Cracked Rear View* (whose title sounds like something *my* mother would have said if someone's pants were riding too low), Hootie et al. provided a minute-long a cappella track of front man Darius Rucker singing our song. Ultimately, it was this version that was successfully imitated by the fellow who landed the solo at my school, a young man, I should add, who went on to a career in musical theatre. But, of course, he had a mom. And with a mother's love as the wind in one's sails, what the fuck can't one do?

As I remember, I auditioned for the solo, too, which really wasn't fair to our choir teacher, the movie-beautiful Mrs. Taylor. If a kid with a dead mom wants to stand up obliviously in front of the whole school and sing about how *sometimes* he feels motherless, you can't let him do that, can you? But you also can't tell him he can't. I guess it's lucky for all of us that Hootie kid came along with his undeniable technical mastery to lift the decision out of Mrs. Taylor's long-fingered, graceful hands. To be honest, although I was by that time just five years motherless, I can't re-call identifying my own predicament in the song's poetry, and it's probably just as well; if I had realized, as a traumatized and sol-ipsistic teenager, that African-American slaves—high in the run-ning for history's most hard-done-by group of people—had been using my *literal* condition as a *metaphor* for their suffering, my already unstoppable self-pity would have gone supernova.

In the end, though, it seems to me that if I wanted to sing the "Motherless Child" solo, they should have awarded it to me on a technicality, Hootie be damned. I would have taken a sympa-thy spotlight; Christ knows I had earned it. Someone who lost their father when they were very young once told me that it was always important to her that other people didn't feel sorry for her, that she wasn't viewed as a charity case, and I told her that I couldn't relate to that at all. There's not even one small part of me that can. I always wanted all the pity that was coming to me for losing my mother. As it turns out, when I got it, it wasn't near-ly enough.

After Princess Diana died, a family friend said to me, quite sin-cerely, that they imagined I must be able to relate to how Prince William and Prince Harry were feeling; besides that seeming, in retrospect, like a bizarre thing to say (unless the family friend were Elton John), it struck me as being the exact opposite of the truth. The whole world—with the exception, one imagines, of some hard-hearted IRA-types and committed American Revo-lutionary War re-enactors—stopped to mourn with William and Harry, acknowledging both their mother and their loss. Every-where they went, for the rest of their lives, people would see them with the tenderness one reserves for orphans and quasi-orphans: the warm indulgence of flaws and failures, bottom lips bit in admiration for all they'd been through. They got to put on a concert in their mother's honour, with her favourite musicians, and everyone on earth got to see it. *Had* to see it.

My mother died in our anonymous stucco house, in a suburb adjacent to Vancouver, on the very edge of the world. If I want people to know her name was Robin, and she loved the Four Tops and James Taylor, I have to tell them. And when I walk into a room telegraphing my neediness, as I invariably do, all anybody sees is a loud straight white man who needs to be coddled even more than an entire society engineered to coddle loud straight white men already does.

My mom, whom I worshipped, who was deeply loving and generous to the people in her life, who was religious in the best possible way and so funny you can't believe it (the same family friend who made the observation about the princes once rightly told me that my mother was much funnier than I: "Like, not even close"), got sick when I was five. Before I turned eleven, she was gone, and in the intervening years she was away from us, in the hospital getting treatment, sometimes for six weeks at a time, sometimes without any warning. That kind of thing leaves wells of fear and resentment deep enough to power whole economies of anger, neediness and insecurity; Albertan tar sands of thick, viscous, dirty fuel for unpleasantness.

For instance: there was a period in my life during which I resented babies. *Resented babies.* Try to imagine the level of anger and hurt it would take for the sight of a cooing babe in the soft arms of his mother to make you think: "Look at that smug little asshole—he doesn't know how good he has it." Happily, this short-lived, unseemly characteristic eventually gave way to an over-identification with any child, anywhere, in need of a parent. Once, because of shingles underneath my wife's breast, I had to bottle-feed my daughter formula in the middle of the night. Her wailing motherless confusion was more than I could handle, and soon I was heaving sobs alongside her.

It is difficult for me to make jokes about death, because in our house it was a terrifying and too-real taboo. When we were kids, no matter how heated a fight got between my brother, Nicholas, and me, we would never allow ourselves to yell, "I hope you die!" even if we desperately wanted to. Instead, the worst we'd let out was the more euphemistic "I hope you get hit by a truck!" I still have great retrospective respect for this loophole, which had all the feigned, outraged innocence of a mafioso on the witness stand: "Hey, woah, woah—I didn't say I hoped he'd die! That'd be totally out of line. I just said it wouldn't bother me if he were hit by a truck, that's all. What happens after that is up to the truck."

My baby brother, thankfully un-struck by any errant semis, was there on March 11, 2011, the twentieth anniversary of my mother's passing. I had asked for a family gathering to mark the occasion, but in the house with my aunts and uncles, I was inconsolable and had to excuse myself. My brother followed me upstairs, trying to comfort me, reassuring me we were not alone, all of our family was there with us. "And they're all here," he said perfectly earnestly, "to celebrate Mom's death."

My brother's innocent slip of the tongue—which made my mother sound like Darth Vader, with jubilant Ewoks dancing around the empty shell of her mask and armour, celebrating the end of her tyranny—melted me into peels of uncontrollable laughter. To be laughing—my mother's first language—with my brother was not enough consolation to stop me feeling like a motherless child. But it did keep me from feeling like I was a long way from home.

My little brother, too, had once sung a slave spiritual. Mom was in the hospital and Auntie Heather gave my brother—who would have been very small back then, with his beautiful voice—the phone. Nicky sang "Swing Low, Sweet Chariot," and my mother listened with love for her second born, this tiny little boy singing into the receiver about bands of angels and the Jordan River, and she thanked him when he was finished. When my aunt came back onto the line, Mom was finally able to release the feelings that she'd kept inside while Nicky was singing: "Can somebody *please* teach that kid a different song?"

N

FOR NAZIS

for Nazis

A FEW YEARS AGO, when my wife and I were in Berlin, we happened to stumble across the former site of Adolf Hitler's bunker (how's *that* for the opening line of the anecdote you least want to hear?). According to what I'd read, the site—some grass, a parking lot—has been deliberately engineered for lack of drama, against the possibility of neo-Nazi memorialization; in the battle against the banality of evil, the best weapon is even more banality. Nevertheless, there is a sign marking the site's historical significance, and when you are there you are fully aware you are standing at the very place where it all ended for history's greatest monster. And if, like me, you are an idiot, you may find yourself filled with a sense of obligation to *do something* about it. Which is why I, seething with anti-fascist courage, *spat* on the *ground.*

Now, if somebody cuts you off in traffic and you catch up to them at an intersection and spit on their car? That's like a nine-out-of-ten reaction. Short of physical violence, it's the most emphatic, hysterical possible response, and it is invariably way too much. Not so, as it turns out, when you're spitting on Hitler. The second you do it, the moment your Allied loogie passes your lips, the puniness of your gesture echoes through all of twentieth-century history. When the target of your contempt is the man who initiated the catastrophe of German fascism and the un-fathomable depredations of the Holocaust, started a war that killed between 40 and 50 million people? *Puh-tew* seems feeble and humiliating as a response. Like if someone broke into your home, killed your whole family, lit the place on fire and then, as they were leaving, you shouted after them: "Hey—screw *you*, man!"

Cara and I loved Berlin. In fact, one of the things that most impressed us was the seriousness and maturity of the city's pub-lic reckoning with its fascist history (it's certainly much more grown-up than the Canadian hugs-then-pipelines approach to our own country's genocidal legacy). If there was anywhere that felt slightly evasive, though, it was the Olympic stadium—a piece of fascist architecture still in use as a sports arena, immortal-ized (in the bad way) by filmmaker Leni Riefenstahl in her propa-ganda film *Olympia* but now featuring gold medal–winning African-American sprinter Jesse Owens with almost hilarious ubiquity as the site's one bit of redeemable history. His photo is everywhere and there's a nearby train station named after him. You can practically hear a sweating German tourism bureaucrat tugging at his collar and saying, "You know, secretly ve vere al-vays hoping zat a black guy vould come und vin everyzing... In fact, you might as vell just call zis ze Jesse Owens Stadium und forget everyzing else, jah?"

Nazi jokes are nearly always in bad taste, yet they seem to be irresistible. In one of his stand-up specials, after an extended riff on Nietzsche and Hitler, Ricky Gervais gives a bad-boy wink to the audience and says, "Not typical comedy material, I'll grant you that." It's a bizarre bit of self-congratulation, because com-edians haven't stopped making Nazi jokes since Charlie Chaplin and Mel Brooks; as far as boundary-pushing goes, they encoun-ter about as much resistance as, say, Hitler did going into Austria (which, for the record, was basically zero, Austria, so you can cut the *Sound of Music* shit).

Karl Marx's famous dictum was that history repeats itself,

first as tragedy, then as farce. It's been pointed out, by writers like Melvin Jonah Lasky, that Hitler reversed this order, with his farcical Beer Hall Putsch preceding his actual ascension to power ten years later. In fact, Nazism—with its kitsch and costumes, its grown middle-class men dressed in stupid boots and armbands, swapping warnings of racial paranoia like recipes, trying to grow the same moustache as their boss—was from the beginning a compound of tragedy and farce. That may explain why humourists can't leave them alone. If the Nazis hadn't done any of the stuff they did, snickering would be the only appropriate response to them. As it stands, they aren't funny, but they can be laughable (or, I don't know, maybe it's the other way around).

To wit: a few years ago, in New Jersey, a neo-Nazi couple made the news when their children, several of whom had explicitly Nazi names, were removed from their care. What does it mean to say that they had "explicitly Nazi names"? It means their oldest child's name was Adolf Hitler Campbell; another was named Joycelynn Aryan Nation Campbell.

Think about that story for a second. At first blush, it is certainly tragic: minds poisoned by fascist hatred, a family ripped apart. But then really think about the details and tell me there isn't something darkly comic about it: they named their first kid *Adolf Hitler.* Look, I don't know any Nazi parents, but I have to believe that most of them would be satisfied with naming the kid Adolf. It's not a subtle homage: "This is our son, Adolf. So... *get it?*" But these two wanted to leave absolutely no wiggle room—or, if you prefer the German, *wrigglesraum*—as to which Adolf they meant. "This is our son, Adolf *Hitler*—remember? It's from racism." Furthermore, most multi-child families have enough trouble with first-born sibling entitlement. How is that problem not going to be exacerbated by having an older brother named after the godhead of the family's whole world view? Naming one baby Adolf Hitler in a brood of young Nazis most certainly qualifies as picking a favourite. How are the *unter*-siblings supposed to feel? My guess is you're going to find yourself with a flock of white-power Jan Bradys in the making (not to mention the girl was named *Joycelynn Aryan Nation*. I'm sorry, but if you are a committed enough Nazi to name one of your children Adolf Hitler? You should be able to name some lady Nazis).

In the end, though, I'm not sure it's the ridiculousness of Nazis that keeps us giggling nervously at them; I think it goes deeper than that. Molière said the heart of the comic was incongruity (one of the reasons spitting on the site of Hitler's bunker is laughable; it's completely incongruous with the enormity of the evil it's meant to gob upon). We flatter ourselves by holding Nazis to be total historical exceptions, wholly alien to us, incongruous with the rest of humanity. We may keep making panicked jokes about them to keep that incongruity alive; the more ridiculous they seem, the less familiar (which is why, when a contemporary fascist shows up on TV in a nice suit, we don't always notice him, and he doesn't make us laugh). In some ways, comedy about the Nazis does exactly the opposite of what edgy humour is supposed to do: it lets us escape any responsibility for, or likeness to, evil. I was listening once to a comedy podcast, where the hosts were giggling over the fact that on D-Day, Hitler apparently slept in until noon. They thought it was funny, but I actually found it terrifying, precisely because of all the things I'd read, seen or heard about the man, this was the first one that I could completely relate to.

for Obsessive-Compulsive Disorder

ONE OF THE CLICHÉS most commonly asserted and accepted about the present state of Hollywood film is that the industry has stopped making movies about the thoughts and feelings of grown-ups to focus, instead, on making superhero pictures. That's a sentiment I have a hard time agreeing with, since the first two movies from which I ever saw my deepest self reflected back at me were *Spider-Man* and *Spider-Man 2*. Tobey Maguire's turn as Peter Parker is as fine a portrayal of obsessive-compulsive disorder as I've ever seen on film.

There have been about a million grown-up movies about people like me—in this case, when I say "people like me," I'm talking about mentally ill people. Pretty much every single one of these movies adheres to what the French writer Emmanuel Carrère nicely called the "romantic cult of madness"; essentially, each of the films I'm talking about boils down to the thesis "You're not crazy, man—the SYSTEM is crazy!" *Well, that's all fine and good*, I would think after watching one, *but my hands are chapped and bleeding from having washed them dozens of times today, and aside from possibly being the work of a shadowy conspiracy by the Purell people, this really feels like it's more my problem than the System's.* "The Man wants to put you in a straightjacket because you see the world a little differently—don't let the conformists shackle your creativity!" *Noted. Now, by "creativity," do you by any chance mean the never-ending loop of images of repellent sexual violence, usually involving loved ones or the vulnerable, constantly flashing in my mind's eye that make me wish I were dead and for which I've developed magical rituals to fend off or cancel out, the execution of which now takes up the majority of my day, every day? Because I am super cool with shackling that.* The healthy, confident idiots who are eager to tell you the whole concept of mental illness is a scam do so almost exclusively from the boneheadedly privileged position of knowing not at all about that of which they speak. They're a bit like the patchouli-doofus tourists who loudly worry that the end of the U.S. embargo will destroy Cuba; they can afford to be romantic about an almost impossible place because they don't have to live there.

Sadly, I did not get saddled with the fun, zany-uptight OCD of the popular imagination. My OCD was a lot less Each-of-These-Cookies-Better-Have-the-Same-Number-of-Chocolate-Chips-or-I'm-Sorta-Gonna-Lose-It-LOL! and a lot more Spending-Almost-My-Entire-Adolescence-and-Young-Adulthood-Wrongly-Worried-That-I-Might-Be-a-Pedophile-or-Will-Somehow-Contaminate-People-Around-Me-with-My-Toxicity. In addition to some of the more recognizable obsessive compulsions (symmetry, handwashing), I had what's called primary obsessions OCD, in which the sufferer is beset relentlessly by invasive thoughts that generally fall into one or several overlapping categories: blasphemy, inappropriate sexuality and violence (an easy mnemonic device is that they're the same three things most young men are looking for in a video game).

In a sick and sort of sweet irony, the content of these thoughts is a reflection of the sufferer's morality. Only someone who loves and would never hurt a child will obsessively worry about inappropriate violent or sexual thoughts about them; my psychologist tells me it often happens with new parents—which is sad, because that's a time in one's life that should instead be spent obsessively worrying about which kind of diaper will kill the planet faster. It's the same with blasphemous thoughts—only a genuine believer would become fixated on the image of taking a dump on a crucifix; an atheist struck by the same notion would either quickly laugh it off or, more wisely, fill out a grant application to do it as a piece of performance art.

As a little Anglican, my first obsessive thoughts were blasphemous. I was a kid, definitely younger than ten, and out of nowhere, my mind would blurt out the thought *I hate you, God!* Since I knew He could read my thoughts, I would race to think something that I figured would be soothing and reassuring for a deity, like *No, I don't. I love you, God.* I was, in short, something like God's crazy boyfriend. My deepest fear was that the first thought, the bad one, was somehow more sincere. This error of interpretation, my shrink says, is at the root of primary obsessions OCD. Everybody has had the horrible stray thought about, say, pushing the old lady on the platform in front of the train as it pulls into the station. Most people dismiss it because they know it's mental detritus. The obsessive-compulsive worries it means something about them, and then they can't shake the image for days, or months, or years. (Which is to say nothing of what the poor old lady herself is thinking—she never gets any agency in this scenario. Whom does *she* darkly fantasize about pushing in front of the train? Probably the kaiser.)

If all that is the *O* part of OCD, the truly fantastical stuff comes with the *C*—the compulsions meant to ward off or negate bad thoughts or bad outcomes. As a little boy, I developed intricate ritualistic prayers that kept getting longer and longer, and if I didn't recite them properly, or at the right times, then bad things could happen. If, for instance, I heard a siren and didn't say the prayer that I was supposed to—which, if I remember correctly, began "Please, Lord, don't let that be for anyone I know..."—then if someone I knew died, it would be my fault. Every *single* time I heard a siren.

Once you've made the initial leap to granting yourself the otherworldly powers to ward off bad thoughts or prevent bad things from happening, it's a short hop to a general outlook of Better Safe Than Sane. Those suffering from OCD have a magical way of conceiving not only their abilities to cause or prevent bad things but also the concomitant responsibilities that come with that—if you *can* stop a bad thing and don't, you're just as guilty as if you'd done it yourself. *With great power,* in other words, *comes great responsibility.* Into this web of anxiety swings your friendly neighbourhood Spider-Man.

Poor, poor Peter Parker—if only he'd been bitten by a radioactive banana, perhaps he'd have all the serotonin he'd need to lead a happy, productive life. Instead, he pores endlessly over the murder of his Uncle Ben, which he believes was caused by his own failure to confront a thief he had no reason (at the time) to believe would kill anyone, let alone his gentle uncle. His attendant overriding grief and guilt have translated into a highly ritualized, stressful and anxious life dedicated to the impossible task of preventing all harm to everyone—just like the homemaker who checks ninety times a day that she's turned off the stove, to prevent her kids' being engulfed in a fiery death, or the guy who washes his hands a dozen times an hour so that he doesn't make anybody sick. Even Spider-Man's superpowers are suspiciously obsessive-compulsive: his "Spidey-sense"—the extrasensory ability to detect the hidden dangers in every situation—is such a blatant OCD fantasy that I'm surprised Howard Hughes never developed it in real life. And who in our psychiatric tribe hasn't spent time climbing the walls?

One of the narrative devices in *Spider-Man 2,* used to indicate the hero's suffocating sense of civic obligation, was that each time Peter Parker heard an emergency vehicle's siren, his eyes would fill with panic and duty and he would speed off to the scene. The reader can imagine, now, why that was such an intimate cinematic moment for me—so much closer to my experience of mental illness than any scene of Jack Nicholson rousing his fellow cuckoo's nestlings to undermine the authority of front line health care workers. As it happens, the first *Spider-Man* was released the year before I came out to friends and family about my OCD; the second, the year after (coming out as obsessive-compulsive is a little bit like coming out of the closet, except that you go back five or six times to make sure you locked it).

It was the summer of 2003 when I finally spoke to somebody about my OCD; I was working a summer job as a groundskeeper, left alone all day with my horror-show thoughts—thoughts that until that point, it had been my life's work to keep secret. But now it felt like they were going to kill me—by which I mean that they were pushing me closer and terrifyingly closer to killing myself. The person I chose to tell was my friend Tej—Tej who was so much taller than me and who was also fatter than me (sadly, no longer true), with a chest-length beard, whose physicality as well as his personality offered countenance and comfort and made me feel small and safe (I don't ever get to feel either of these things). I don't remember what I told him, except that I had something important to confess, and we ended up in some field on or near Burnaby Mountain that is so brilliantly green in my memory I know I can't be remembering it exactly as it was. I started telling him about the images, the intrusive thoughts— the mental reels of the most graphic and nauseating violence, of predation on little babies and children, all the things that had me worried I was pure evil and unredeemable darkness. Before I could finish, he enveloped me. The deep sympathy in his face, the hugeness of the chest and arms that he took me into—they were the first real release I'd felt in years.

Everything that came after that—the therapy that transformed OCD from the omnipresent, driving terror of my life to something I've basically moved beyond, with occasional flare-ups at times of high anxiety—was possible because of his response. On my wedding night, Tej was driving my brand-new wife and me to our hotel and, along the way, chauffeuring my incredibly drunk mother-in-law to where she was staying; as she got out of the car, she turned to Tej, whom she had just met, and told him she loved him and thanked him "for being in our lives." We still tease her about it to this day, but in fact, she had chosen the receptacle of her affection wisely. (Incidentally, on that same ride, she also drunkenly demanded I acknowledge my marriage to her daughter could never have happened if it weren't for Pierre Elliott Trudeau.)

So, Spidey is not, in the end, the superhero of my OCD story; that role is filled. Still, I could see myself in him, and that meant something. "Wherever there's a hang-up," the old song goes, "You'll find the Spider-Man." Oh, I've got hang-ups. I'm your friendly neighbourhood obsessive-compulsive.

for Panic

FOR THE FIRST few days after my wife and I brought home our newborn daughter, Joséphine, from the hospital, a shrill kettle-whistle shriek of panic rang through the house almost non-stop. Our third night home, for instance, I awoke to the terrifying sound of breathing coming from deep within my pillow and began desperately pawing at it like a meth-addled Norfolk terrier until I realized in all likelihood I'd been dreaming, and the baby probably wasn't inside. My overtired wife, Cara, contributed to the general hysteria the next night by waking me to desperate pants of "Where's the baby? Where's the baby?" after she had (a) noticed that Joséphine was missing from her bassinet and (b) forgotten that she was in the midst of breastfeeding her.

When we shared these stories with well-meaning friends, they kindly assured us this was just part of being a new parent, like stroller-related status anxiety and the mythological status of sexual intercourse. Although that may have been true in Cara's case, I knew better with regard to my own anxieties. Because although they had now found a new, admittedly more adorable subject upon which they could be projected, there was nothing unique about them (okay, the stuck-inside-a-pillow thing was a novel spin).

But I had already been on internal, wide-eyed hypochondri-acal death-watch-without-respite many times before, frozen stiff with neuroses, then convinced it was rigor mortis. There was the half year I spent working on a reality TV show, over the course of which I lost many pounds, mostly by throwing up (and not only because I was working on a reality TV show). That year, I became convinced that I was allergic to every food and medi-cation that passed my lips—pursed, as they were, in a rictus of worry. The most consistent exercise I got in those days was run-ning through the various tests for stroke. Complaining alternate-ly of light-headedness or chest pains, I visited the ER more often than most people see their GPs (probably more than most people see their parents). Incidentally, besides my socialism, my hypo-chondria is one of the reasons I never complain about kicking in tax dollars to pay for universal health care; I've had cardio stress tests that turned out to be for little more than my undershirt be-ing on backwards.

This firmament of generalized worrying has, over the years, been punctuated by more acute bouts of panic. The first time I can remember having a legitimate panic attack was in grade ten, during an afternoon classroom screening of *Koyaanisqatsi*—an aversion to avant-garde film that took an early medical turn. I remember the constant low-humming repetition of the title against the Philip Glass score whipping me into the sort of vague but terrifying panic normally reserved for Adam Sandler movies. I acted out in class, drawing attention to myself even more dra-matically than usual, having no idea what was happening, which didn't stop me from getting in trouble. I've never revisited the film and have often wondered—does he get the girl in the end?

The next attack happened almost ten years later, in the com-munity hall on a Secwepemc reserve outside Kamloops. Dozens of us had driven up from Vancouver for a solidarity action with First Nations activists opposing the expansion of the Sun Peaks ski resort onto their traditional traplines. (It's only fair, I guess, that if I'm bringing up the Secwepemc's objections to the resort,

I should present the other side of the argument too, so here goes: "Skiing is fun! Also: *ka-ching!*") We would all be spending the night in sleeping bags in the community hall before heading to the resort in the morning. I don't know if it was the thought of bunking in a single room with the entirety of Vancouver's hard left or just settler guilt gone nuclear, but something triggered that same all-encompassing but impossible-to-pin-down *Koyaanisqatsi* jangle of nerves.

I excused myself to take a breath outside, sat in the passenger seat of my friend's Mustang and before long I was bawling. As embarrassing as the tears were I had no language to explain them to the friends who came out and found me. In a stroke of white-guy luck, the pal I was there with had a family cabin on Shuswap Lake, less than an hour's drive from the reserve. We drove to those more private accommodations, where his parents were already staying and where I could quietly wind down, then wake up to a breakfast of homemade waffles and waterfront view before heading off to our confrontation with colonialism. For someone who has, as I've said, no higher aspiration in life than to one day become a bona fide champagne socialist, it was pretty close to a perfect day.

It takes a special kind of male twentysomething idiocy not to follow up on an incident like this. To walk away from a dizzying *ex nihilo* crying jag without any curiosity about why it happened seems something like saying, "Well, that was unpleasant—let's hope that next time I eat shellfish, my throat doesn't inflate like a Zeppelin!" before digging into another surf and turf. Instead, the panic attack that finally forced me into addressing them as an ongoing medical problem took place in just the place where you'd expect an inveterate leftist to be driven to the brink of hysteria in those pre–Naheed Nenshi and pre–Rachel Notley days: Alberta.

I was on the road as a touring opening act stand-up comedian for the first time in my life and had spent several days in the sort of personal health–related panic I had become an expert at over the years. Over the course of my days, I have alternated between periods of being what you might call pretty fat and what you might call very fat, and this was during a very fat phase. Standing in a sports bar in Lethbridge, where we were supposed to do a show despite the fact it was NHL playoff season, I felt a pain in my left arm (in retrospect, probably it was just my soul trying to escape from my body). I became convinced I was having heart problems. A day or two later, I found myself in a hotel room in Calgary in the middle of the night, suffering from what appeared to be a heart attack. All the signs were there: my arm felt funny, my chest hurt, my pulse was racing and I had pizza sauce all over my face.

Now, there are several reasons why one might find oneself having a heart attack in Calgary. Perhaps you're David Suzuki, or a vegan, or a bull. But I am none of these things, so I decided I had to get to the emergency room, where I could get on with the business of dying. Riding to the hospital, I kept stealing glances at the taxi driver, who was a moustachioed ginger—and although this should have comforted me, as it made him a composite of what my redheaded mom and French-Canadian dad looked like when I was a kid, it didn't. Instead, I kept thinking, *This is the last person I'll ever see. This is the person with whom I end my life.* It didn't even make me feel better knowing that, by dying, I'd get out of paying the fare.

Inside the hospital, I placed terrified phone calls from the waiting area to my brand-new wife, trying desperately to telegraph my love and hysterical terror through the payphone, across the Rockies. Lying on a bed inside the ER, I plumbed new depths of fear, facing down eternity with even less confidence than I had taken to the stage earlier that week after contracting to do significantly more time than I had material to cover, before crowds who could generously be described as indifferent. I stared up at the ceiling of the hospital, plunging into more fear than I had the resources to deal with, so I turned to humanity's oldest circuit breaker: for the first time in my adult life, retrieving the religious language of my Anglican upbringing, I prayed. Like the solipsist in every myopic faux-damascene conversion story, I prayed hypocritically to a God I hoped would forgive me for my until-that-very-second atheism and spare my life. I begged Him to save me. And a few seconds later, a nurse wheeled an EKG machine into my area, hooked me up to it in what seemed like one fluid motion, told me I was perfectly fine, then disconnected the machine and disappeared. After that, a doctor explained I had had a panic attack. By the time I left, I'd been acquainted with two of humanity's great soothers of the soul: prayer and Ativan.

Invariably, relief follows the discovery that one has had a panic attack rather than a heart attack—even though the phrase "panic attack" is made up of two profoundly terrifying words, whereas the phrase "heart attack" is only one terrifying word, qualified by one of the most comforting words in the English language. So on paper, panic attacks are worse. But heart attacks can kill you; panic attacks—as horrifying as they are—cannot. For this reason, the initial response to finding out you have panic attacks is often relief—followed by disappointment at the realization that, although you get to live, you may be doing so with chest pains, dizziness and diarrhea. But in my view, panic sufferers needn't view themselves as shaky, shitty people. Instead, we should see ourselves for what we are: paragons of evolution, the ultimate culmination of Darwinian natural selection, in all of its horror and brutality.

Just as twenty-first-century toddlers with access to corn syrup are weighing in at three hundred pounds because Cro-Magnon man had a hard time finding sugar and fat, the problem of panic is a physiological one rooted in the differing circumstances between us and our remote caveperson ancestors. As much as they make one feel like a weenie, the symptoms of panic attack each bear evolutionary advantages related to the fight-or-flight instinct, also known as the Air Canada Imperative. When faced with a sabre-toothed tiger or a she-wolf, our hunting-gathering ancestors generally had two options: they could stand and fight, or they could run away. These vestigial instincts are still apparent in human behaviour today. When you respond to stress by acting like an asshole, that's fight. When you respond by acting like a coward, that's flight. When you write something mean in an internet comments section, you're doing both.

Fight-or-flight was a crucial survival system, yet it has bequeathed us both anxiety disorders and panic attacks—the symptoms of which usually correspond to an evolutionary survival mechanism.

Let's take an easy and relatable one to start: excessive sweating. Those suffering from panic will often begin to sweat profusely and disgustingly. But according to the website for AnxietyBC, a West Coast mental health resource website (meaning it's just like the mental health resource websites in Toronto but less ambitious or career-focused), the evolutionary advantages to profuse sweating are obvious: "Sweating cools the body. It also makes the skin more slippery and difficult for an attacking animal or person to grab hold of you." Incidentally, we may just have stumbled upon the very worst superpower of all time.

Panic attacks often involve rapid heartbeats and a constriction of the chest—but these are merely fight tactics, with blood being pumped to the major muscle groups and chest muscles tensing for battle. Chest pains, sweat, heavy breathing—these are the hallmarks of a warrior, and that's why there's nothing scarier than a sixty-year-old businessman who's just had to take the stairs instead of the escalator.

The list goes on—panic sufferers often feel a sense of reality seeming less real, also known as the Tea Party effect. Again, according to AnxietyBC, this is because of the dilation of the pupils to let in more light. Sexual and gastrointestinal dysfunction come from the body de-emphasizing non-essential systems in a time of crisis, which to my mind raises the question: What exactly do we mean by non-essential? That said, if you're being chased by a bear, it's probably better not to have an erection—not only will it be easier to run, but you'll seem like a smaller meal.

So why don't people know more about panic attacks? Partially, it's because we panic disorderees don't really have a celebrity spokesperson. Our leading contenders, the two most famous sufferers, are Tony Soprano and American actor-comedian Jay Mohr. One of them makes his living by means none of us should condone; the other is a fictional New Jersey mob boss. But perhaps the most obvious contender for the public face of panic is staring right at us: Charles Darwin, the cousin-marrying visionary who outlined the process of natural selection that screwed us over in the first place.

Over the years, religious fundamentalists have taken issue with evolution because of its godlessness, its rationalism and its use of the words "bone" and "erectus." I would argue they have missed the number one cause for complaint: evolution sucks. It's left some people with connected eyebrows, others with a fear of monogamy—and me? I'm constantly dizzy, peeing and clutching at my chest.

For those readers who may think this is a pretty weak conclusion for an essay, I'm trying to make a point about evolution: things don't always get better or build to greatness. So, you know. Think about it.

Q FOR QUENTIN TARANTINO'S USE OF THE N-WORD

for Quentin Tarantino's
Use of the N-Word

MOST OF WHAT I need to say on this subject has already been said better by Spike Lee, so let's keep this short. There's nothing more grating than the white guy who chimes in with "I agree, and here's why, in twice as many words..."

It's hard to overstate the importance *Pulp Fiction* had on my arrival at something like cultural maturity. Released in my mid-teens, it was the first hip, slightly inaccessible cultural artifact that I understood and experienced in real time. Watching it wasn't like trying to sneak into a jazz club underage or tittering at a pair of upturned black-and-white nipples in a European movie; to be a fifteen-year-old getting high and watching John Travolta stabbing a syringe full of adrenalin into Uma Thurman's chest after a milkshake felt exactly right, an aesthetic moment I understood all the angles and contours of but wasn't yet bored by. When a gym teacher chaperoning a band trip down to Portland refused to let us watch the tape through our bus's onboard TV/VCR system, I remember feeling, more than anything, a puff of superior bemusement.

My friends and I so loved *Pulp Fiction* that when our grade ten drama class required us to put on a short play, we instead transcribed an excerpt of Tarantino's breakout script and mounted a multicultural theatrical rendition of it (something like Jason Schwartzman's character in *Rushmore* did with *Serpico* a few years later). I got to play Travolta's Vincent Vega; my friend Basilio, who had done the painstaking (and often incorrect) transcription, was an Italian-Canadian Samuel L. Jackson; tall, thin, half-Scottish and half-Japanese Alex played Harvey Keitel's The Wolf; and half-Filipino, half-indeterminate-European Chris was stuck with Jimmy, the put-upon, hapless-in-housecoat friend-with-good-coffee played by Tarantino himself.

Tarantino has been criticized not so much for using the n-word but for rattling on it like a kid banging drumsticks on the dinner table: it's unnecessary, it's artless and it seems to be more about drawing attention. His language in general is pyrotechnic, so any live junior high production of *Pulp Fiction* would have to be seriously bowdlerized, of course, and we lost a great swathe of f-words and s-words and such. One of the lines that we had to censor was delivered by Chris as Jimmy, who, in the film, holding a cup of his outstanding coffee and with great emotional understatement, asks his friend, who has just brought a corpse to his home, whether there's "a sign outside my house saying dead [n-word] storage?" Instead, Chris asked, first plaintively, "Is there a sign outside my house that says dead guy storage?" then raised his voice: *"Is there a sign outside my house that says dead guy storage?!"* It was the only line in Tarantino's movie that was better with our edit.

for Rats

FULL DISCLOSURE: THE FOLLOWING passage will make my childhood seem a lot grittier, more urban—say, tenement-like—and less supervised than it was. I am not trying to claim a greater share of street cred than I am due; I was as herded, cloistered and surveilled as any other post-Clifford Olson suburban North American child, and neither I nor any of the neighbour boys hawked newspapers or dodged streetcars or had tuberculosis. Nevertheless, the following is true.

One year sometime in middle-childhood (say seven, eight, or nine), the week after Halloween, my brother; my best friend, Shaun; and I found a dazed rat beside the curb in front of our houses. I don't completely trust my memories of this rat's face, which seem to have melted into my memories of the original live-action *Teenage Mutant Ninja Turtles* movie, with its large senescent rodent *sensei* puppet, Splinter. I do remember, though, that the rat's narrow head was moving enough that we knew it was alive and confused, but otherwise, it had been robbed of the scurrying fleet-footedness that is normally a rat's greatest asset.

We began debating the best next steps, and it was immediately clear that opinion was split. Although he wouldn't admit it outright, Shaun clearly favoured some sort of assisted suicide, or at least torture, but since my brother and I were such sensitive boys, he knew that he had to dress it up as caring. "The best thing would be to hit it in the head with a brick, to wake it up," he suggested a little too eagerly, and at that point lost his political capital. I suggested we do what we could to nurse the rat back to health. Since our trick-or-treating bags were still full of the lesser handouts that generally manage to survive into the first week of November, we had a ready supply of sunflower seeds. If I remember correctly, we also filled an upturned yellow Frisbee with water for the rat to drink (though, again, I may be confusing this memory with the time Shaun and I peed into an upside-down Frisbee as part of a booby trap). Whatever the case: we brought the rat food and drink, crouched next to the curb to make sure it got both (thankfully some sort of proto–common sense stopped us from touching it), and afterwards, I left feeling we had done the right thing.

Our treatment worked; the rat was able to get its bearings and leave the curb. I know this to be true because the next day, a two-dimensional version of the rat was lying in the middle of the street, a few feet from where we had found it. For some reason, none of the adults on our block saw fit to sweep or shovel the flattened corpse away; it just lay there until the birds and the rains slowly erased it. Every day, as we got into the car, I would see less and less of it, and it was like a boring ghost that made me about five years more cynical every time I saw it. *Well, that's what I get for trying to help; we just got it killed,* I would think, uncharacteristically keeping to myself, rather than sharing with my parents, the details of our rescue mission. Then one day, finally, it was gone. Nothing lasts forever, even cold November rat.

As my curbside Florence Nightingale heroics indicate, I was fearless of rats as a little boy. Contrarily, I was terrified of spiders. I was so obsessed with the thought that they would crawl into my bedsheets as a kid that my mom told me if they touched anything that had been bleached, spiders died immediately; it wasn't until years after she died that I realized this was a protective fib.

For a long time, before I could sit on a toilet, I would have to lean my head practically into the bowl to see if there were any spiders underneath the rim, waiting for my bum to be steered as cluelessly into their trap as a fly into a web. In my late teens, I moved into the basement of the house we rented and never once worried that I was sleeping next to the unfinished storage area our landlords used, and where they had seen fit to lay out a bit of prophylactic rat poison. In contrast, I couldn't even bring myself to kill the large wolfy, grey spiders that shared my cooler, darker part of the house; I would instead chase them away with a container of hairspray whose contents I would spritz through the flame of a lighter to create a fireball. (I imagine, had anybody known about this tactic, my landlords might have seen an increase in their fire protection premium.)

Now here's the part I can't explain (or, in light of the preceding fireball confession, maybe I should say, here's *another* part I can't explain): at one point, in my early twenties, rats and spiders swapped places in my encyclopedia of fears and anxieties. I don't mean to say that gradually I got less afraid of spiders and slowly became more wary of rats. It happened all at once, like someone turning a switch. And although there is a zero-percent chance this could actually be the reason, and there is no scientific explanation for how this could be, and no way to reproduce these results in a laboratory, I will state, for the record, that I clocked the change the first time I ever took antidepressants.

I am telling you the facts: I took Paxil for a couple of months, after which I was no longer afraid of spiders and suddenly skeeved rats. Today, I am the kind of person who sees a spider in a corner of the room and, if he or she seems respectful of the space and isn't being a dick, will shrug it off and count the insects they're killing as rent. Just recently, I brought my baby girl close to the spider's web that's been hanging peacefully between our front porch light and deck chair for several months, introducing its architect as though they were an old friend. Conversely, a few years ago when I was leaving the house for a late-night walk, a rat jumped from underfoot as I passed my neighbour's chicken coop, and I had to leave by the other side of our housing complex. I still can't think of it without my spine almost collapsing from tingles.

More recently, public health authorities have targeted the blocks around our co-op for rat control. Two blocks from where we live, there is a community garden lot at a busy intersection; it sits across the street from our favourite restaurant. One summer night, as we were finishing a late dinner just after the sun set, I saw a group of rats milling and socializing with a confidence that suggested they'd just gotten out of a seminar. I was far enough away from them that I wasn't panicked, but I was stunned—it was the exact same energy you might see at a dog park on a busy weekend, only in miniature, unsupervised and plague-riddled; dozens of them of all sizes, just as relaxed and confident as you please. Relaxed, that is, until an owl—the first I'd ever seen live in my life—dropped down from a tree, grabbed a long submarine sandwich–sized *Rattus* from the pack with its talons, then gracefully disappeared backwards as though being rewound, scattering the rodent party. (And here I should say, where earlier I had to disclaim that I never lived in a Sergio Leone, *Once Upon a Time in America* New York shtetl, I also don't live in a David Attenborough nature documentary.)

I'd never seen anything like it; a little while later, I was telling my aunt about this community garden swimming with vermin just a stone's throw from our house, and she said, yeah, she'd heard about it on the news. *On the news.*

So okay, maybe my life is just a *little* bit gritty.

for Settlerism

I HAVE A SOMEWHAT more romantic view of the city of Winnipeg than do most Canadians (who aren't Guy Maddin or my friend John K. Samson). This is owing to the exclusive way in which I have experienced the city, namely, as a guest of the Winnipeg Comedy Festival, which happens to be one of the best in the country, takes place in post-polar/pre-mosquito April and puts us comics up at the chi-chi Fairmont hotel overlooking Portage and Main—what I'm told is the windiest intersection in the country, or maybe it's the world, but anyway, I've never found the statistic particularly compelling (why should intersections provide the evaluative framework for windiness? It seems like a random, haphazard sample selection, like offering the median income only for men named Steve). I've been lucky enough to attend the festival several times and have a great relationship with its director, so I eagerly answered yes when he phoned me in my swank room at the Fairmont right after I'd arrived one year to ask me to do him a favour: there was a show that night at one of the theatres, and there was no one there to give a welcome on behalf of the festival before the program started and to introduce the evening's emcee. Would I do it? I'd be happy to, I told him. The show was an all–First Nations lineup of comics, performing for a mostly Indigenous audience; in the name of the festival, I was to thank them for being there and pass things over to them for the night. It was, I am convinced, the first ever historical instance of a white man's being asked to do a ceremonial acknowledgement before kicking off an all-Indigenous program.

The energy in the room as I took the stage was tentative, not suspicious but wary—which is not necessarily a function of racial politics, and is in fact how the lion's share of comedy shows begin in any context. I introduced myself as being from Vancouver, unceded Coast Salish territory, which was the widely accepted protocol I was used to. I couldn't tell if the unsteady vibe in the room owed more to my whiteness or to the fact that I hadn't yet ventured a big joke, so I made a plunge that for most stand-up comedians is instinctive: I tried to deflate what I perceived to be the biggest tension in the room.

"As a white comic," I said, "I love performing with my First Nations colleagues. Because if I like any of their jokes? I can just steal them." The response was immediate: huge, warm, relieved. Emboldening: "And then I'll tell everybody that I discovered them—'Hey, look at all these jokes I found! No, I'm not a joke thief, I'm a joke explorer!'" The rest of my short set went very well. I got to slip in a line about the Hudson's Bay Company, which had recently stolen the design for Cowichan-style sweaters, thus besmirching the company's otherwise immaculate record of relations with Indigenous nations. When I handed things over to the evening's emcee, he cast a kind eye back on my act, saying "Coast Salish? Cowichan? Not bad... for a white guy."

What I didn't know at the time was that the evening's host was a polymath activist / rapper / journalist / writer / broadcaster who was just trying his hand at comedy and who would become something of a household name (in the right kinds of households but households nevertheless built on stolen land): it was Wab Kinew, and he was funny. I also didn't realize, as I was backstage kibitzing with the other acts, that one of the guys I met, Ryan McMahon—a Winnipeg-based Anishinabe-Métis stand-up and graduate of Second City—was on the verge of breaking out as a bona fide anti-colonial comedy sensation, ceaselessly touring the country on a self-invented circuit bearing no resemblance or relation to the ones in the conventional (white? settler?) comedy world. Whereas the rest of us tend simply to go wherever the clubs are, or the bars with once-a-week comedy nights, Ryan has spent the past years finding his audience, wherever they happen to be, and getting to them. Ryan and I would go on to become close friends. By the time I made a later visit to Winnipeg with my wife, we were intimate enough for me to complain to him about the difficultly of having sex on the ultra-soft Fairmont mattresses, right after the act that may have been my daughter's conception.

Winnipeg came under fire in a 2015 cover story in *Maclean's* magazine titled "Canada's Most Racist City"—there is not a lot of ambiguity in that title, but keep in mind that Winnipeg isn't big on subtlety or prevarication; the city's rich neighbourhood is named Tuxedo. On the Canadaland podcast, editor and media commentator Scaachi Koul pointed out that the headline drew attention away from the litany of brutal abuses, poverty, targeted violence and racism enumerated in the piece; instead, it had kicked off a conversation about whether Winnipeg was, in fact, really the worst. The spectacle of an entire country built on genocide and dispossession arguing over which part of it was most racist ended up being a little bit like asking, "What's the Cheesiest Part of Wisconsin?" only way grimmer.

When I was growing up, my sense was there were broadly two attitudes or understandings about the Indigenous nations in what we now called Canada: (1) the mean right-wing idea that we had destroyed them, but this wasn't something to lose much sleep over or (2) the generous liberal idea that we had destroyed them, and this was a real shame and we ought to think about it every once in a while and try to be nicer to the few Indigenous people who were left. In other words, the two understandings were identical except in terms of attitude, and the consensus was that, whatever had happened, the notion of an Indigenous future was off the table. The idea that Indigenous peoples might instead become the fastest growing demographic in the country, with legal and political rights that might affect our compulsive need to dig up or pump out whatever's in the ground and ship it out like lunatics breaking up the furniture in someone else's house to be used as kindling—that didn't seem to have occurred to a great many of us.

We were the couple of generations of white-skinned Canadians who had come to understand that our responsibilities with regard to the eradication of racism began with tolerating exotic music, venturing increasingly spicy recipes and might in some extreme cases extend to material largesse in the form of social programs and affirmative action jobs. As it turns out, this training left us relatively ill-equipped to deal with the grievances of First Nations, Métis and Inuit, who seem less interested in finding a hyphenated, subcultural Canadian identity and more interested in exercising their legitimate sovereignty over the land. Meanwhile, it's becoming increasingly clear that having a resource-based economy in a country where the treaties that exist have been ignored and abused, and where vast swathes of land had no treaties to begin with, makes Canada one enormous morally relaxed pawnshop.

The country is being forced into a reckoning; I'm happy to see it, because I know we wouldn't have gotten there ourselves. And although I love Winnipeg, I won't defend it against the serious accusations that have been made against it—except to say that the question of who is most racist is about as compelling or important as which intersection is windiest. A much more difficult but important question to ask is whose land that intersection was built on in the first place.

for Tax Rage

A FEW YEARS AGO, fast food–style accounting firm H&R Block ran a thirty-second spot that achieved every advertiser's dream: it became part of the zeitgeist. In the commercial, an embarrassed young man complains of ass pain (the implication being, in case any of this is too subtle, that that's where he's been fucked); the no-nonsense medic, taking a quick look and pulling a long wince, throws up his hands and says, "That's tax pain. Nothing I can do about that."

To run a commercial, in Canada at least, that frames anti-tax grumbling in a doctor's office is, if nothing else, ballsy. At least the kid isn't going to have to pay for the visit. There's a certain amount of cognitive dissonance in making a character who theoretically would be paid in tax dollars the bearer of tax-weary cynicism—like having a police officer explaining, "That's tax aggravated assault, I can't protect you from that" or a firefighter saying, "That's tax fire, I'm afraid your family is destined to be engulfed in flame."

Taxes, though, share the rarefied rhetorical position of terrorists and sex offenders as being the universally detested evils plaguing liberal democracy (this despite the fact that everything done to keep you safe from, or to punish, terrorists and sex offenders is paid for with taxes). They are unquestionably bad. Decrying taxes is no longer seen as remotely ideological; it goes completely uninterrogated, like saying, "Cookies are quite pleasant" or "Kickboxing is not for newborns."

Every year, the Fraser Institute, a prominent and well-funded right-wing think tank, celebrates Tax Freedom Day, the average date by which most Canadians have earned out the taxes they will pay that year and thus begin "working for ourselves," keeping all the money—presumably money they minted themselves that hopefully wasn't stolen by brigands in the midst of their nightmarish, stateless Hobbesian neighbourhoods. Incidentally (and this is true), to enter the Vancouver offices of the Fraser Institute, it is first necessary to pass through a Bentley dealership. The battle for the "common sense" around taxes has unequivocally been won by the right. *What it comes down to is this,* we've heard time and again, *Who spends your money better: You, or the government?* The question is always posed as though the answer is obvious.

Here's the thing, though: not only do I believe the government spends my money better than I do; the competition is not even particularly close. In my home you will find: a treadmill, purchased brand new from Canadian Tire, which I have used *maybe* six times; the complete 1960s *Batman* series on DVD; any number of fruits and vegetables at various stages of spoilage in the same kitchen as recently emptied takeout containers. I have paid for music on the internet. And I see evidence everywhere I go that I am not alone in my profligate idiocy; we live in a society in which grown men and women spend hard currency on bottled water, spa days for canines and artificial testicles for their trucks.

I've never once come home drunk, then opened my laptop and impulse-purchased a school or an ambulance; I've also never impulse-commissioned a piece of avant-garde theatre or poetry. My friends have never come over and helped me build a road for pizza. We've never all kicked in a few bucks to have Rex Murphy come over and lecture us about things (although from what I've read, it does actually sound like this might be an option).

The assumption is always that taxes are a loss, but the Canadian Centre for Policy Alternatives—a think tank at the other end of the spectrum from the Fraser Institute, of which I am a supporter and whose annual fundraiser gala I host, and into whose Vancouver offices one may ascend not through a Bentley dealership but through a phalanx of pot smokers spilling over from marijuana activist Marc Emery's flagship head shop—came out with a 2009 study that suggested otherwise. According to the CCPA report, median-income Canadian families enjoyed public services worth 63 percent of their income. Admittedly, you've got to weigh those services against the freedom to build your own school, with textbooks that explain how dinosaurs built the pyramids and with math questions that never end with the number 666, but it's pretty impressive.

Taxes, as the old saying goes, are the price we pay for civilization. You know it has to be an old saying, because no one would ever have said something so lucid about taxes and the collective good in the past thirty-five years—since at least after the election of Margaret Thatcher. Perhaps Mrs. Thatcher's most infamous quote was her pronouncement that "there is no such thing as society." Her conservative fans often complain that this phrase has been shorn of its context and made to sound cartoonishly super-villainish, so here's a fuller version, from the *Spectator*'s website:

> I think we have gone through a period when too many children and people have been given to understand "I have a problem, it is the Government's job to cope with it!" or "I have a problem, I will go and get a grant to cope with it!" "I am homeless, the Government must house me!" and so they are casting their problems on society and who is society? There is no such thing! There are individual men and women and there are families and no

government can do anything except through people and people look to themselves first... There is no such thing as society. There is a living tapestry of men and women and people and the beauty of that tapestry and the quality of our lives will depend upon how much each of us is prepared to take responsibility for ourselves and each of us is prepared to turn round and help by our own efforts those who are unfortunate.

Thatcher-lovers seem to think that fuller context makes the Lady sound better; the *Spectator* blog framed the quote as "What she *really* said about society." I tend to think it's the opposite. Sure, maybe on a quick pass, one thinks, *Oh, okay, it's not as harsh as it sounded at first,* but then after a few seconds, it's *Wait... that's way worse.* (First of all, "too many children"? Holy *fuck!* If a kid has a problem, and their parents can't fix it, then whose job is it to take care of them if not the government's? Santa's?)

When, like me, you grow up with a sick parent, the simple and ideological division of the world into a public sphere and a private one seems deeply flawed from the get-go. From the time she got sick, when I was five, until the time she died, when I was ten, almost every moment I had with my mother was in some sense a public good: she was able to be at home because of long-term disability payments; she was treated in a hospital by public sector care providers and with technology bought and paid for with tax dollars. As most people grow up, they realize their parents, their families, are not only not all-powerful but are in fact relatively powerless and can offer precious little besides emotional support by way of defending against the vagaries of fate and the wide, cold world. The presence of illness and death in early childhood drive these hard lessons home much earlier and much harder. There are individuals and there are families, as Mrs. Thatcher said, but there are a great many things they will be helpless to deal with on their own. But one of the great things about human beings is that something like economies of scale kick in for us as well, if people are willing to pull their weight. There are things we can do together that most of us couldn't do for ourselves.

Since ancient times, the only way to afford a civilization has been either to tax one's citizenry or else to brutalize and exploit foreign, semi-colonized people in the far-flung corners of the earth. This may be naive, soft-hearted and sappy, but: I believe Canada can continue to do both.

U FOR
UNION-BUSTING

for Union-Busting

IN FILMMAKER FRITZ LANG'S 1927 masterwork, the titular Metropolis is a city divided (as well as a city resplendent with a love-robot who could also be described as "titular"). Underground, an army of poorly paid and anonymous proletarians trudge lifelessly to endless shifts of back- and soul-breaking toil, along with, one assumes, acute vitamin D deficiency. Above ground, "so deep as lay the workers' city below the earth, so high above it towered" the glittering pleasure palaces of the rich, where fortunate sons engaged in what we can only assume was Weimar Germany's vision of perfect idyll: shirtlessly foot-racing against other young men or chasing elaborately dressed concubines around a massive hanging garden complex. As the sons sow their wild, Teutonic oats, the capitalist fathers of Metropolis rule the city with a utilitarian cruelty. Although the film has a certain Marxist science fiction, class-struggle-in-space vibe, it is, upon closer viewing, essentially a reformist ode to religious stoicism and Keynesian reconciliation: "The mediator between head and hands," goes the film's refrain, referring to bosses and workers, respectively, "must be the heart!" It doesn't say anything about bosses who are, say, pricks or assholes.

In the suburb where I grew up, though, Metropolis was the

name given to a new wing built onto the local mall. My home-town of Burnaby was no exception to the widespread banality of North American mall culture of the 1980s and '90s, with its murky, clouded skylights and food courts buzzing with neon and deep fryers. In 1986, as I was attending grade one just a few blocks away, Metrotown mall landed in the South Burnaby eco-system like an invasive species, transforming everything around it (not least my school, student enrollment at which quintupled over the next decade or so). Metrotown became the central geo-graphical fact of my life: it was where we saw movies; it was where we bought the groceries; it was where we visited the li-brary; every bus or train I took passed through its transit hub; it was where I first saw sushi; it was where I first ate sushi; it was where I would continue, for many years, to eat sushi. We played soccer and baseball on fields right next to it, took swimming les-sons in a rec centre not two hundred feet from one of the mall's many entrances. When my father finally, reluctantly gave up the right to cut our hair at home—a privilege he had not relin-quished even after accidentally snipping off the tip of my ear—it was where we were barbered.

But the once-dynamic Metrotown, with its stationery stores and its RadioShack, seemed positively sleepy compared to the new outgrowth horseshoeing from its north side after 1998: Me-tropolis, a funky, brightly lit expansion that included a lush, chirping novelty restaurant called Rainforest Cafe; the greasy, forced joviality of T.G.I. Fridays; a nerd-focused boutique done up in a faux-brick castle, selling crystals and warlock statues; a shop selling gourmet site-made and hand-spiced potato chips; and an ominous movie megaplex called Famous Players Silver-City. Metropolis also housed a thumping, bleeping, cavernous arcade called Playdium (I'll give a parenthetical pause here for the reader to allow the full cleverness of that name to wash over them), a garish complex whose company literature eschewed the humility of what it called the "a-word," opting instead to be known, in a fit of late-'90s corporate euphemism, as an "LBE," for "location-based entertainment" complex. In retrospect, it's difficult to see how the phrase "location-based entertainment" couldn't just as easily be applied to a strip club or a cockfight.

This was our Metropolis. However, just like its namesake in Lang's silent black-and-white classic, this was a pleasure dome rife with subterranean class antagonism occasionally bubbling up to the surface.

Before the end of its opening year, in December 1998, local 348 of the International Alliance of Theatrical Stage Employees (IATSE), the projectionists' union, was locked out of Cineplex Odeon and Famous Players cinemas across British Columbia, including at SilverCity Metropolis. With changing technology ostensibly de-skilling projectionist work and making it less dangerous, the companies were moving to break the union. For months, Metrotown's proud new experiment hosted a feeble two-man picket line at the bottom of the escalators leading up into the theatre. As armies of ticket- and popcorn-buyers blew past nonstop, the union members were like flickering two-dimensional projections: images easily ignored. Once a week, my schedule unburdened by, say, team sports or sexual relations, I would walk the picket line for a few hours in the evening, handing out information sheets to uninterested and unmoved passersby. Now and again, from the base of the escalators, my eyes would wander curiously over to Playdium down the hall. I had no way of knowing that in a few months, not only would I be working there but it would become the site of my own little quixotic battle in the eternal struggle between capital and labour, head and hand, Donkey Kong and Mario.

At age nineteen, in the spring of 1999, after leaving behind life in the Trotskyist sect in which I had spent my adolescent years, I was on the cusp of university life and looking for a job to complement my new and petty bourgeois student schedule. Having opted to leave the party to pursue higher education, I had also opted for the possibility of (in fact was counting on) a transition back into the dread middle class, even just the lower echelon in which I had grown up. I was therefore free to leave the dirty, dying grown-up world of factory and warehouse labour for the cushier children's crusade that was work at the mall.

I took a job at Playdium as something called a Playmaster— this was my official title, though it is an economic category that will not turn up in even the most exhaustive search of Marxist class struggle terminology. Playdium itself was a whirring coliseum of kinetic sensual explosion: beeping game consoles and virtual reality simulators, thumping music, smoke machines, an IMAX theatre with moving seats mounted on hydraulics, a restaurant in which orders could be relayed through an onscreen virtual waitress (then delivered by someone in an organic body), a bar overlooking the suburban skyline and a gift shop, in case one worried they were in danger of letting the memories of their magical visit slip through their joystick-palsied fingers. At least one game—a horse-racing simulation that involved riders, often women, straddling the trunk of a plastic horse that would go faster and faster the harder the rider pumped and jiggled—seemed like it could only have been designed by a sex offender. If I had to describe Playdium in one word, the word would be "throbbing." Engineered to irritate and arouse the senses, the enterprise was staffed almost entirely by young people in their physical primes, with the magma of post-adolescent sexuality surging invisibly under everything. Since I had so recently come from the mostly older, mostly male world of blue-collar labour, the amount of sexual electricity in the air at Playdium threatened to break my circuits. I'm not proud to admit that I was stumbled upon in the bathroom of the men's change room at least once in the midst of—how to put this delicately—palsying my fingers around my joystick.

For the most part, I loved my new job. But as novel and leading edge as Playdium tried to be, this was still capitalism; this was still Metropolis. There were indignities typical of any other service industry job staffed mostly by young people, along with some that were, as far as I know, unique to our workplace. The money was bad: just a few cents an hour more than minimum wage. The hours were odd—not only running late into the night (4 AM on Friday nights) but also disbursed in seven-hour shifts. Since the threshold to qualify for benefits was thirty hours a week, anyone working fewer than five shifts—like any of us who were students—were disqualified, but anyone working the full five shifts a week still wouldn't be getting forty hours. We Playmasters received one unpaid half-hour break per shift; those who worked in food and beverage service had been told frankly that, on a busy day, they might not receive any break at all. There were unpaid but mandatory pre- and post-shift meetings, and if any worker had the temerity to take precautions against the deafening robot orgy into which they'd been hurled, they were informed that earplugs were not part of the uniform.

More idiosyncratic, and slightly more humiliating, was the Playdium "sock check," in which a manager would shout out, "Sock check!" forcing the assembled employees to hike up their pants to demonstrate they were wearing the appropriate hue of stocking (black). The kitchen contained a Wall of Shame— photos of employees who had worn the wrong colour of socks. These rules were enforced as arbitrarily as they would have been by Cesare Borgia; I once saw a young woman lift her pants to reveal bare feet tucked into her shoes, as the manager collapsed into peels of good-natured laughter. The same manager once solemnly told a young man who had yanked his cuffs up to show a pair of white tube socks that he wouldn't be allowed to work that day because his uniform was incomplete. As I remember it, this issue was resolved when I lent the young man a pair of my dirty black socks—though as my labour history professor told me when I relayed this story, "Seems like the sort of memory one might well repress."

Now, as the old saying goes: you can take the Communist out of the League, but you can't take the League out of the Communist (okay, maybe nobody's ever said that, but it happens to be true). My natural inclination was to read all of these indignities systemically, and as any good working socialist knows—whether your job is felling trees near a logging camp or Windexing the sweat of a hundred strangers off the goggles of a virtual reality hang-glider simulator—our only weapon against the bosses is organization.

My first sense that I might have an ally in rallying the class war troops was on a drive home from work with Pardeep. That's not his real name; since he was also our drug dealer, I've decided to give him a pseudonym. Pardeep's profile didn't immediately suggest "potential union radical." In addition to his entrepreneurial proclivities, his father had been a failed candidate for the hard-right, populist Reform Party, back in the days before it had transformed into the more respectable Conservative Party of Canada and tamed some of its hostility to... well, people the shade of Pardeep and his father, for one. But Pardeep was charismatic and well liked, a fun guy to be around, and his job working the cash register in admissions had rankled him with its lesson in the production of surplus value, and he complained on that drive home about how little we all were getting of the seemingly massive cash flow that he was processing every day. After some initial trepidation on his part, I convinced him that we should meet with organizers from the Canadian Auto Workers—it was my old union, and after all, one of the biggest draws at Playdium was an Indy 500 machine.

The men at the union hall gave us a stack of salmon-coloured union cards and told us that if we could get 55 percent of our co-workers to sign them, our workplace would be automatically certified (meaning without a second vote). We had to be careful, however, to keep our bosses in the dark for as long as possible, or else the inevitable management counter-offensive would start too early. Pardeep and I entered Playdium that afternoon like giants, the confidence of assured victory nestled in our hearts. As I dressed for work, I slipped one of the union cards into my (black) sock, and headed for the IMAX, where Brian, a young man who'd been told repeatedly that his earplugs were not part of his uniform, was working. He signed the card. I didn't tell him it had just been up against my foot.

Between us, Pardeep and I knew the lay of the land in admissions and among the Playmasters, but the food and beverage department was alien territory. Based on his quiet, thoughtful countenance—which was so anomalous at Playdium that it was like a massive flashing neon sign—I decided to approach a young man named Carlo, who worked at the snack counter. Carlo was still in high school; he was an East Vancouver kid whose mother was from the Philippines and whose father was a Holocaust survivor who had escaped Europe with one of Raoul Wallenberg's fake passports. Over coffee, I showed him my hand and explained that separately we workers were just vulnerable fingers, but together we made a fist. And since there was no screenwriter present to erase what I had said for being hackneyed and cliché, the analogy stood and won young Carlo over to the union.

The weeks that followed were some of the most exciting in my young life—Pardeep, Carlo and I embraced the cloak-and-dagger aspect of the organizing drive, hiding cards on our persons and sneaking them among the game consoles. We called ourselves the Buffalo Soldiers, since we stored our cards in two-compartment Buffalo brand pencil cases; one compartment for unsigned cards, one for signed. Since we were joining the Canadian Auto Workers, the CAW, employees in the know would signal one another by flapping their arms like wings and yelling, "Caw! Caw!" (okay, "cloak-and-dagger" isn't precisely the best way to describe screaming like a crow at your co-conspirators). We drove to people's houses with cards to be signed (sometimes with a ziplock bag full of mushrooms in the glove compartment that Pardeep had to deliver to a client). The Buffalo Soldiers would give late-night, impromptu lessons on workers' rights in the downstairs parkade or in the Dunkin' Donuts that sat a cruller's throw from work. In the end, we exceeded our target by almost 20 percent and were automatically certified with 73 percent sign-up.

And that's when that management counter-offensive we'd been warned about got started. Historian Orlando Figes wrote about the Soviet Union: "In all revolutions there comes a moment when the high ideals of the revolutionaries crash onto the hard rocks of reality." To put it in more Playdium-friendly terms: there comes a time in every game of Frogger when you get hit by a fucking truck.

It's easy to feel like you're winning if your enemy doesn't realize that a fight has started. During the secret phase of our organizing drive, it was as though we had allowed ourselves to forget that, in the final analysis, we were a gaggle of suburban teenagers who worked in an arcade (or location-based entertainment complex). Management's opening negotiating gambit was a disorienting one—they hired a team of labour lawyers, both named Barry. From the double-Barry onslaught forward, the bosses never lost momentum.

The union's negotiating committee consisted of the assigned union reps from the CAW, the Buffalo Soldiers and our newest comrade, Elecia. None of us had known Elecia very well before; I don't even think she'd been one of the 73 percent card-signers. But she was a couple of years older than the rest of us and was acutely embarrassed to be working in an arcade. She had taken to the union with energy and anger.

We faced off against management and the Leather Barrys, as we'd christened them in honour of their ludicrous matching leather bomber jackets (honestly, if you work with a guy who has the same name as you, twin rules apply: you can't wear the same thing). The Leather Barrys unleashed a flurry of stall tactics, offering less than the status quo on certain clauses of the contract, the legal bare minimum (even for non-union workers) on others. We were blindsided by post-Christmas layoffs that targeted senior, union-friendly workers and spent a great deal of energy scrambling to get them rehired. The longer the bosses made us wait, the more support for the union ebbed among our young, fickle co-workers. Our union rep, a not-so-gentle giant named Roger (who had no other Roger to work with, but who, with his massive height and weight, pretty much counted for two people anyway), alerted us to a byzantine corner of the provincial labour code that would allow us to go into mediation, but only if we took a strike vote. We did, and although we received a majority mandate, it was a weak one. Donkey Kong kept raining barrels on us from above, and we didn't even have a hammer.

Absurdly early into the mediation, Playdium tabled a final offer. The contract didn't contain any language on the sock check, which may have signalled a small victory. But that was the only one in there. We urged our members to vote no, which a little more than a third of them did; just less than a third voted yes; a plurality of them didn't bother voting at all. This despite the fact that on the day of the vote, our general manager was featured in a front-page story in the *Vancouver Sun*, discussing the company's wild success and plans for expansion.

Faced with the prospect of going on strike with less than a third of the staff behind us, I blinked. I could see the whole thing unfolding in my mind's eye, along the same tragic lines as the projectionists' lockout: brisk business booping and bleeping behind us, customers and co-workers shrugging off our easily ignorable picket lines. Over Roger's initial protests, we decided to decertify. Game Over.

The day the decertification went through, Carlo and I, who'd become close friends, went into Playdium with our uniforms folded crisply underneath our resignation letters. We refused to work one shift in the newly non-unionized LBE; instead, we both took jobs even lower in class war esteem: as parking valets with a service contracted by luxury restaurants across Vancouver. I think Pardeep started promoting electronic dance music nights in clubs, keeping him fairly close to the *esprit de Playdium*. Elecia got a job at a gym—or, if you prefer, location-based exercise complex.

As it turns out, the braggadocio in the newspaper had been mostly bluster—it wasn't long before the company began contracting, and soon the Metropolis location was shut down. The distinctions between Metropolis and the rest of Metrotown mall have since levelled off, and the space once used by Playdium was taken up by the decidedly unhip department store Winners, a poetic little reminder that in a zero-sum game like class warfare, they're the only ones left standing.

V FOR VALET PARKING

for Valet Parking

IF YOU ARE a reeling nineteen-year-old left-wing radical having a crisis of faith because your union-organizing campaign has been crushed by the forces of reaction, may I strongly recommend that you do not immediately take a job parking and retrieving the luxury sedans of the wealthy as they dine out, in restaurants you'll never be able to afford, at the height of the dotcom boom. Not all, maybe not even a majority, of the rich people you meet will be terrible. The actor Beau Bridges, for instance, will be incredibly kind; one night, on his way into dinner he'll tell you, "I cheated. I parked my own car tonight" before giving you a $5 bill anyway. But in the end, you will hate most of them, and you will hate yourself.

Class status is a slippery concept in a place that pretends it doesn't exist, like North America. When I was very little, my dad sold suits and, like my mom, worked dispatch for the RCMP, making them both public sector union workers (though eventually Dad became a manager at the suit shop, so who knows where that slots him into the eternal struggle between labour and capital). When my mother got sick, she went on long-term disability, and Dad continued to work dispatch as he went to school and trained to be a teacher; after Mom died and Dad was a single parent teaching full time, he went back and got a master's degree, then taught until I was about seventeen years old before becoming first a vice-principal, then a principal. It was a complex hybrid of a working- but mostly lower-middle-class upbringing: we never owned a house, but we went to the symphony and watched productions of Shakespeare; it felt like we had less cash but more cultural capital than some of the blue-collar people we knew. True to stereotype, Dad's then-still-secret homosexuality tended to mean that we had pretty nice stuff, but my brother and I also ate more boxes of Kraft Dinner than have been purchased with the money from every student loan ever made.

Further complicating my formative sense of class identity was my adolescent contact with rich people. The first sustained interaction that I ever had with people who had money (at least more than we did) was in my early teens, when our family friends— who also happened to be our landlords—would invite us to their waterfront summer cabin for the friendly annual tennis tournament they held with their neighbours on one of the Gulf Islands off the southwest coast of British Columbia.

If you're a kid who's never met any rich folks, allow me to recommend waterfront summer tennis tournaments as a great place to start. One of the friends I made on the island, Nicholas, had a "cabin" with a ping-pong table and a hot tub overlooking the ocean; he pointed out once that the questions I was always asking about money (I hadn't realized I'd even been asking them) suggested that I was obsessed with it, but I think that's pretty typical when someone who doesn't have any connects with someone who has a lot. Our friends-and-landlords' youngest son would announce to my brother and me that when he grew up, he would kick us out of the house we were renting from his family and claim it as his own. This young man grew up to be a very sweet and wonderful person, just like his parents, who to this day continue to welcome my family and me to their cabin. I love them all to bits, and I think they'd laugh at my characterizing them as "rich"—and in the scheme of things, they may not be.

Back in my youth, as I became a champion high school debater, I got a further peek into the lives of youngsters who, like me, were nerds, only *affluent.* Through various tournaments, I came to know all sorts of private school kids—the sort of kids who in September asked each other "Where did you go this summer?" instead of "Where did you work this summer?"; kids who were going to Harvard and Stanford, who were heartbroken on the odd occasion they were only accepted at a Canadian university; kids whose parents pulled me aside and asked me straight-faced why I wasn't applying to Yale.

It was easy to be envious of these summer cabin friends and prep school debate colleagues, but there was never any reason to hate them. They certainly weren't the reason I was a high school communist, and besides my occasionally tweaking them a little with a bit of white-baiting (reverse red-baiting) now and again, that was as far as our class conflict went. I fancied my socialism as a cool, detached, historical thing, not driven by rage or pettiness. Apparently, the radical *Nation* columnist Alexander Cockburn used to ask all the magazine's interns, including future British Labour Party leader Ed Miliband, "Is your hate pure?" as a way of testing their mettle; Miliband apparently answered that he didn't hate anybody, and before I became a parking valet, that's probably the answer I would have given, too. But things change.

I worked for a service called Park Avenue Valets—after Playdium, I promised myself I would only work for employers with puns in their names—which had contracts with a number of upscale restaurants throughout Vancouver and its suburbs and would also take contracts for private events. Before my first shift, I went to Walmart (shopping alongside the last sorts of people I might encounter in my new career) and bought a white shirt and $11 bow tie. I wore them underneath the work-issued red vest and I was, I have to tell you, beautiful. For most of my life, I have at best been called cute, but this was something else. At the beginning of my valeting days I was temporarily thin and muscly, and I had my blond hair in a buzz cut. When I arrived to my first shift, my boss, Joe—a very sweet East Vancouver Italian guy who worked for the city and operated Park Avenue on the side—looked at me for a long second before saying, "You look good," then repeating himself, "You look *good*," the way men do when they want you to know you look like the lady in that Eric Clapton song. That first night, the maître d' and the chef of the restaurant where I was working came out onto the front stoop just to admire me. It felt wonderful.

But after that, unless I did something wrong, I effectively disappeared. In our vests and bow ties, we valets were basically interchangeable, figures of contempt when we figured at all. One night, I had the wind almost knocked out of me by the punishing indifference of another maître d' at a different restaurant. I had gone in to ask about something, but before I had a chance he turned to me and said, without irony, "What do you want, *boy?*" I couldn't speak, I was so taken aback. Halfway through my sentence, he turned on his heel and walked away. Nobody had ever been that rude to me before in my life (because unlike the private school kids, I had never been to Paris).

I don't think I was the best valet there ever was. On my first shift at what was then a happening new seafood restaurant, I went to retrieve a blue Mercedes from the underground parking lot, checking my blind spot as I backed out of the stall before crumpling the other side of the vehicle into a concrete pillar (the car's owners, a very sweet old couple from Alberta, were understanding; the Evangelical security guard informed me that he had "said a little prayer" for me when I crashed, so that may be why). But I learned how to be *fairly* good at the job by following one rule: whatever felt most dignified, I would do the opposite. I once sang for a tip. When it rained, I'd never stand under cover because the wetter and more pathetic I looked, the bigger the gratuities. One fellow among a group of travelling businessman gave me a $20 bill because I pretended I hadn't noticed him puking drunkenly into the garden I had to stand beside for the rest of the night. Occasionally, I would lash out peevishly and immaturely against my own surrendering of self-respect: I'd make a big show of reading Gramsci outside the restaurant so that people would know I had a brain (until one of my Chomsky books was stolen while I was parking a car). I farted in a vehicle once, right before I brought it back, and although it was an accident, Freud said there aren't any, and I can't say I felt any sharp regret. But soon enough, I'd go right back to forfeiting my respectability, nodding through instructions from a higher-ranking car-parker about the "huge" difference between parking a Bentley that belonged to a board member of the Fraser Institute five versus ten feet from the front door.

The one bit of dignity that I clung to was my refusal to deliver on the unspoken expectation that I would shoo panhandlers away from the front of the restaurant. When your job is to stand on the street, parking fancy cars outside fancy restaurants, pretty much the only people you interact with are the rich and the homeless, and for each group, you represent the bridge into the other world. A local BMW dealer pulled up once in a z8, what I was later told was about a $300,000 car, and asked me to park it someplace safe: "It tends to attract," he said, darting his eyes side to side, "flies." Many times, I watched people who'd just spent hundreds of dollars on dinner come out onto the sidewalk and mock panhandlers for laughs from their families. I refused to tell the street folks to move along. There was one guy who would do one-armed push-ups for spare change from giggling plutocrats, but I mean, how different is that, in the end, from standing in the rain on purpose?

I had once hated the vast impersonal system of capitalism, but working as a valet made me hate individual capitalists, personally. I felt my politics more viscerally, and resentfully, than ever before but had less and less of an outlet for them. I sank into resigned, seething, lonely despair. In the end, though, I really needn't have felt alone, because a few months into the job, George W. Bush stole the U.S. election, and pretty soon it felt like we were all valets running errands for plutocrats, and everybody was just as resigned, seething and despairing as I was.

Except, I assume, for Beau Bridges. That guy has a fantastic attitude.

for The West Wing

THERE'S PROBABLY NEVER BEEN, in my lifetime, a raising and dashing of hopes as historic and as precipitous as the one bound up with the first, say, six years of the Barack Obama presidency. There've been ones more historic—the failures of liberal democracy to take hold in much of Eastern Europe after 1989–91, or of peace and brotherly coexistence in Israel / Palestine after 1993, or of multiracial socialism and equality in South Africa after 1994 were all *bigger,* but they unfolded in tragic slow motion, and the Cassandras who'd insisted on grounded pessimism in the first place were only vindicated in retrospect. There've been ones more precipitous—just a few seconds into *Star Wars: Episode 1,* for instance, most of us had the terrifying realization that we had elevated a thorough mediocrity from our childhoods into soaring epic; but that wasn't necessarily *historical.*

But Barack Obama, as the first black president elected by a country built on a chalky bedrock of white supremacy, the leader chosen after a combination of End of History and End Times thinking had lit the world afire with borderless war-making, then exploded the economy with the frantic sugar-rushing-boys-in-a-clubhouse gamesmanship of a Pokémon session, had a multitude awaiting enormity from him. And instead, he sucked almost immediately. In the sunset of his second term, there were once again a few discernible shimmers of what people had Hoped for, with, for example, marriage equality (though he'd originally opposed it) and the disorienting, rushing sounds of sanity entering foreign policy discussions about Iran and Cuba. On top of that, the people who hated Obama most viciously were just so vile, hateful and racist that many decent folks were inclined to come to his defense (Winston Churchill was a reactionary dick, but if Mussolini had called him fat, I'd have had his back). Nevertheless, the policies and personnel of the first years of the Obama administration were marked by a greater level of continuity than there was between, say, *Late Night with David Letterman* and *Late Show with David Letterman*. And when Obama became the first president since Kennedy to act like a person towards Cuba, Guantanamo Bay was still the conspicuous site of a Kafkaesque outpost of imperial ugliness. Even the great disappointment to come after Obama, the Arab Spring, was muted by the fact that it took place in the long shadow of his mighty sucking.

Both critics and defenders of the president made the point that it was unfair to have expected radical change from him: both his record and his rhetoric placed him squarely in the tepid centre. This observation, like the fact that my younger brother is so much better looking than I am, is simultaneously true and unfair. It was pretty obvious, in the lead-up to the 2008 election, that Obama's multi-hued and multi-generational army of supporters—many of them voting either for the first time or for the first time in ages, either because they were that young or they had been that demoralized by the pre-Barack political world—expected him to Change things (where'd they get that idea?), and nothing was done to disabuse them of this notion. Sorta, you know, the opposite.

That said, there was a text available by which astute observers could and should have foretold that whatever American liberals did to replace George W. Bush, it was going to stink—that it would basically involve all the same anti-democratic impulses, secretiveness, American imperialism and extrajudicial killings but with better speeches. This text would allow one to take liberal centrists at their word, their ideal scenario fantasy-making, and see that even then, the best they could come up with was hot garbage. And this text was Aaron Sorkin's executive branch soap opera, *The West Wing*.

I didn't personally have the benefit of this Sorkinian prophecy, having failed to even once watch the program during its initial network television run, from 1999 to 2007. In 2014, however, fifteen years after it first aired, the program became available on Canadian Netflix. Buried in work and having just become a father, it seemed like a good time to stop everything and catch up on my late-nineties/early-aughties American ephemera.

From early on in its run, the show was broadly seen as a weekly, ritualized liberal fantasy of a world where George W. Bush had lost the 2000 election. And as it turns out, that fantasy looked remarkably like the world where George W. Bush had won the 2000 election: anyone who had the temerity to question the logic of corporate free trade or the American two-party system was still held up as a figure of ridicule; savage, atavistic Arabs were still in need of juiced-up American foreign policy to keep them in line ("They'll like us when we've won," says a character with whom we are meant to sympathize). There was always a broad swathe of American liberalism whose chief complaint about Dubya was that he spoke like a man who'd been bitten by a radioactive turnip—move the speechifying dial from NASCAR to NPR and they'd be happy. That's just what *The West Wing* did.

Admittedly, sometimes things in make-believe president Jed Bartlet's world went in exactly the opposite direction as they did under not-quite-reality-based president Bush, but this generally had more to do with Sorkin's deeply flawed (or mendacious) portrayal of the nature of American power in the world. President Bartlet goes out of his way to stand up for the legitimately elected president of Haiti when he faces a *coup d'état;* his chief of staff laments that a palace revolution in Venezuela has brought the U.S.'s chosen candidate to power, because "process mat-ters." Both these episodes aired shortly before the United States abetted armed right-wing thugs in overthrowing the govern-ments of Haiti and Venezuela. Watching them is a bit like when O.J. Simpson said he was going to go after the real killers.

If *The West Wing* had been produced by any other country, it would be held up as an example of that national culture's pe-culiar authoritarian impulses. If the Germans, say, had created a show encouraging us to root for a plucky band of mostly un-elected technocrats as they struggle against the besieging mass of stupidity that surrounds them—managing shit-ignorant civil-ians too brain-dead to understand the tininess of their concerns or objections, outsmarting the members of a free press who don't seem to realize how lucky they are to have the minutes they get to take dictation, shutting down political allies and opponents for failing to show sufficient fealty to presidential power—we'd probably be talking about the power-worshipping streak running from Bismarck and Nietzsche through Wilhelm and Hindenburg to the failed artist in the brown shirt. But we're not talking about the land of Martin Luther; it's the land of Martin Sheen, and he's so damned avuncular most of the time and slightly squinting ser-ious when he needs to be that, instead, we're meant to swoon.

We know we're supposed to swoon because we're told to swoon, just as we are told exactly how we're supposed to feel about everything we see on *The West Wing*. In an episode during season one, for instance, we are repeatedly told, by several char-acters, that we are going to see press secretary C.J. Cregg per-form "The Jackal," and that it is the greatest thing that we will ever see. "Don't ever talk to me during 'The Jackal,'" says grumpy, im-possible-to-impress communications chief Toby Ziegler, so we know it's good. Craggy, hard-boiled chief of staff Leo McGarry, who usually floats above any comic relief on *The West Wing*, en-thuses child-like about "The Jackal"—and Leo usually only gets excited about aircraft carriers, so now we really know it's go-ing to be something. When the mythic "Jackal" turns out to be nothing more than the underwhelming sight of a white woman lip-synching to a black woman, well—if we're nonplussed, we're left with the impression that somehow that's our fault. Leo and Toby love it.

It's even less impressive when the show has black people lip-synching to white people—specifically, Aaron Sorkin. Canadian cultural critic Jeet Heer has written about the "racial sock-puppetry" in Joe Klein's U.S. political novel *Primary Colors*, whose black narrator espouses his white author's views on African Americans. Sorkin does Klein one better. When, a few episodes in, the show's first black lead is introduced—Charlie, who will become the president's personal aide—Sorkin's script is defensive about introducing a token black character, essentially in the role of a butler. In fairness, as the series continues, Sorkin and actor Dulé Hill flesh Charlie out, making him a human. But being didactic-in-the-wool, Sorkin can't leave us to discover that. Instead, he has various white characters biting their nails about hiring a black manservant, before the president finally runs it by one of his high-ranking (but relatively bit-playing) African-American military advisers, Admiral Fitzwallace, "Fitz," who asks the president in his manly voice, "You going to hire this young man? Pay him a fair wage?" before informing the president (really us, the audience) that there is no problem with it. Hey, thanks Totally Fictional Black Man All of Whose Words Come from Aaron Sorkin for letting us know there's nothing to worry about here, racially speaking.

We're guided, with a pair of heavy hands, towards forgiving other bits of racism along the way. In one episode, C.J. laments that, because of affirmative action, her teacher father always lost his promotions to less qualified black women, and she suspects his dissatisfaction with where his career ended up may be the reason he is now developing dementia (which reminds me of the old joke: Guy goes to the doctor's office, and the doctor says, "I've got good news and bad news." So the guy goes, "What's the good news?" Doctor says, "We're addressing centuries of white male privilege and the oppression of everyone else by levelling the playing field with affirmative action." Guy asks, "What's the bad news?" Doctor explains, "You've got Alzheimer's." To which the guy goes, "Oh well, could be worse, at least it's not affirmative action.").

In a famous post-9/11 episode, "Isaac and Ishmael," Leo makes no effort to hide his racial-cultural animus against an Arab-American White House staffer who may or may not be a terrorist, telling the young man in the context of an interrogation, "That's the price you pay..." before trailing off. When we find out the young man isn't a jihadi, Leo makes something like an apology, admitting that the end of the "That's the price you pay" sentence was going to be "for having the same physical features as criminals." Then, just as he's finished explaining to the young fella that if he asks around the office, people will tell him that the outburst was out of character, Leo realizes that, despite having been given the fifth degree in his workplace for reasons of racial profiling, the young man has continued at his work. "Way to be back at your desk," says Leo, with genuine you're-all-right-kid gravitas as Sorkin invites us all into the warm bubbling hot tub of post-racial neo-liberalism, where white men are still always the ones in charge but people from the other, crappier genders and ethnicities have every opportunity to redeem themselves through the act of constant labour.

The jarring sexism of Aaron Sorkin's oeuvre (not jarring like what simple, honest womenfolk do with fruit preserves while important men make vital social decisions but jarring as in unpleasantly surprising) has been widely decried. Most of the criticism has been directed at his jowl-wobbling tribute to mansplaining, *The Newsroom* (a show that also, sadly, relegated the much better Canadian sitcom of the same name to the status of *"The Newsroom*—not the HBO one but the Canadian *Newsroom*"). But *The West Wing,* too, has all the gender-political sophistication of an episode of *The Newlywed Game:* a man orders a woman to sit and take dictation and the scene is played for laughs; the same woman is later trying to win the heart of a different man, who violently smashes an ashtray with a monkey wrench right in front of her to prove a point (about Pentagon procurement, no less—silly broad!); the president humiliates a trusted female staff member by forcing her to wear a silly hat and sing football songs on Air Force One; a man sexually harasses his co-worker, only to be defended by that same co-worker when a shrill and probably lesbian bit player points out that sexual harassment has just taken place; a female character comes to expect that the very important campaign manager who never remembers her name is never going to remember her name, when all of a sudden she smiles because he's bought her a necklace with her name spelled out in gold—which is an extra non-sexist gesture, being so unlike a dog collar.

The necklace bit is emblematic of *The West Wing,* because it's both cynical and sentimental—the two poles between which every second of the show alternates. Many observers have criticized *The West Wing* for being smug and sanctimonious, but worse than that, it's also treacly, and smug and sanctimonious about what it chooses to be treacly about. The prejudices and preoccupations of everyone outside the White House are ridiculous, but huge sections of especially the first two seasons are devoted to heavily scored scenes in which the characters stand in quiet awe of the United States of America or of themselves. The show is like one of those commonsense pundits who manages to be both smirking and stentorian, giggling through whatever he thinks is the silly self-righteous ritualism of the politically correct but at the drop of a hat waxing mawkish over Vimy Ridge or anti-communist literature.

As I got further and further into the series, more and more angrily my wife would ask me why I kept watching it. Since we weren't ourselves on *The West Wing,* I couldn't just tell her to shut up and take a memo about how brave astronauts are; I felt like I needed to offer an explanation. The fact is, the show is intensely watchable. Partly, it's about how well put together it is, how beautifully designed and choreographed, how well acted, how, from a certain perspective, well written.

But there's more that makes it so watchable: when you first start taking it in, there's an undeniable feeling of forward momentum in every episode that makes the viewer feel like they're headed for something big. Even during boring moments, you feel like you're on the verge of seeing something that will change everything.

Yet more often than not, the Epic Showdown or True Test of Grit or Big Political Battle never materializes. The president has been lying about having multiple sclerosis, and there's going to be a big life-or-death showdown with his opponents in Congress— but then, there isn't. His doctor wife, who treated him in secret, is set for the battle of her lifetime to keep her medical licence—but then she pre-emptively gives it up. We meet Bartlet's Neanderthal Republican opponent in the general election, the two men hissing and barking at each other with carefully restrained, then carefully released malice and drama—then the only time we ever see this guy again is for a couple of seconds in an episode where we already know the president is going to win re-election.

The West Wing keeps kicking the ball down the field in terms of the action, the big confrontation with antagonistic forces— and in that way, it couldn't be a more perfectly liberal, centrist show. The illusion of forward momentum to hide the fact that nothing's going on and nothing ever changes—why else do you think the people most likely to tread water, satisfied with only occasionally tweaking the status quo, always call themselves "progressives"? Yes We Can, they explain to you, before adding smugly, We Just Probably Never Will, and here's why you're an idiot for wanting us to.

X for XANTHAN gum

for Xanthan Gum

IN THE VAST preponderance of alphabetically organized lists, the entry for *X* is almost invariably terrible—either one of the few English words beginning with *X* is somehow shoehorned into service despite its being completely inappropriate, or else the rules of the list are relaxed to make way for a term that simply has *X* in the first syllable. I remember once sitting in a doctor's office and staring up at an ABC poster full of obvious or cornball medical advice ("B: Be Active!" or "W: Walk to Work!"), yet the entry for *X* still managed to stand out in its total garbageness: "X: X-Ray and Examine Problems." Now that's eXtremely eXcremental writing.

So I was more than a little intimidated by the tough job of choosing an entry for *X*—there are very few things that begin with *X*, let alone bad or awful or terrible things that begin with *X*, and rarer still bad or awful or terrible things that begin with *X* and of which there are humorous observations to be made. The obvious frontrunner would seem to be xenophobia—a genuinely terrible phenomenon that has a way of drawing out tragically funny, dim-witted behaviour and utterances from its practitioners, the xenophobes. Furthermore, xenophobes themselves often like to try their hands at particularly crude jokes. In fact, xenophobia and a certain kind of comedy have a long history with each other; they go together like xylophones and xenon. An essay on xenophobia would, therefore, present ample opportunities for a cool, decent, ironic and non-racist humourist like me to make racist jokes that couldn't *really* be racist because I self-identify as cool, decent, ironic and non-racist. Any white hipster worth his Himalayan crystal salt will tell you there's plenty of comedy gold to be mined in them thar ambiguously racist hills.

Nevertheless, I've chosen the seemingly benign polysaccharide xanthan gum. Produced in a fermentation process that combines apparently kind-hearted bacteria with plant sugars derived from corn, soy or wheat, xanthan gum is not particularly funny, and there is no consensus whatsoever that it is terrible. Bob Moore—the gentle, smiling, white-bearded and cap-wearing man whose face brands the Bob's Red Mill line of natural food products—called xanthan gum "one of my most wonderful and most unusual products... of all the natural food ingredients in the world, this powder, when combined with liquids, makes the most wonderful viscosity. Folks, it's just about the gooiest, stickiest stuff there is." So: why xanthan gum?

If byzantine coffee orders were the *sine qua non* of yuppie obnoxiousness ten years ago, today it is byzantine lists of food allergies (followed closely by the use of terms like "byzantine" and *"sine qua non"*). If a contemporary screenwriter wishes to instantly establish a character as being flighty, out-of-touch, self-centred, big-city, unwholesome, unsympathetic and anti-proletarian, they need only have that character squeamishly refusing good, honest, Just Folks food because of an allergy. When I first started dating my wife, who brought with her a long list of genuine food sensitivities, I watched this populist cynicism for food allergies play out with server after server, in restaurant after restaurant. She was aware of it, so she would wince as she tried to order in such a way as to avoid the foods that would pass through her system like a band of marauders. Her chief allergy was to wheat, which, being a heavily subsidized and deeply Canadian grain, came with a certain ubiquity among industrial foodstuffs; if you think you've seen embarrassment, try watching a Chinese-Canadian woman, as she sits across from her white lover, tell a waiter in a Chinese restaurant that her body can't handle soy sauce. (Please note: this last sentence was *not* cut and pasted from an abortive draft of the "Xenophobia" essay.)

The social antipathy towards those with food allergies is hard to resist; even though I loved her, I would sometimes lose patience with my wife's gastro-allergenic needs. I even briefly considered taking a mistress—not for anything sexual, mind you, just somebody I could share dinner rolls with. Turns out, though, it was a good idea not to open that particular line of karmic credit, as not long after, I was diagnosed with my own litany of verboten victuals.

In those days, I was working in a writers' room to which one of my very lovely colleagues would bring bags of home-roasted almonds. After eating a handful one day, I noticed that my cheeks were slightly puffier than their usual already-pretty-puffy. Nut allergies are nothing to trifle with (unlike an allergy to trifle, which can be easily dealt with by avoiding eating dessert with WASPs), so I was sent to an allergist to be tested. The results were a mixed blessing: although I wasn't allergic to nuts, and could, therefore, safely travel to baseball games without an EpiPen, I did have allergies to apples, oranges, bananas, rye, egg whites, cow's cheese, rice and corn.

Let's review the list—the first thing you'll note is that I'd lost each and every one of the convenient fruits. In North America, if you need to quickly grab a piece of fruit, 98 percent of the time it will be an apple, orange or banana. Convenience stores don't carry bunches of washed grapes; kiwis and pears are sold rock hard, as investment fruits. When faced with an allergy to apples, oranges and bananas, one has to develop a relationship with alternative fruits, like pomegranate, which is a fruit that absolutely refuses to meet you halfway. I once complained to a friend about the inaccessibility of pomegranate, and he pshawed me, then sent me a four-minute YouTube video on how to open one with "ease." *Four minutes.* In my opinion, a successful fruit ought to be something a monkey could smash open on a rock and begin scooping immediately into its maw; I believe that any fruit that comes with a four-minute instructional video will always be a bridesmaid.

A rye allergy cuts out most of the great deli foods—the less said about the time my wife and I pathetically shared a plate of breadless smoked meat at Schwartz's in Montreal in the middle of the night, the better. An egg-white allergy means I can never fully relate to guys who like to work out (an alienation that, to be fair, was probably cemented earlier by my myriad earlier life-style choices). And cow's cheese, well—qualifying it like that, as though cows were just one of myriad delicious cheese-producing animals, is even more cruel. Cow's cheese is just cheese, where-as cheese from a goat has to be qualified as goat's cheese, in the same way that wealthy, famous American comedians win some-thing called the Comedy Awards, whereas relatively unknown, underpaid performers north of the border win something called the Canadian Comedy Awards.

The heavy hitters on my list of foods to be avoided, however, were rice and corn. Rice was embarrassing; go back to the earlier scene of the Chinese-Canadian woman explaining to the waiter that she can't have anything with soy sauce in it; now imagine her white lover following up with "and I can't have *rice.*" The cultural inconvenience of this allergy really cannot be overstated: I mar-ried into a Cantonese-speaking family, and the Cantonese phrase for eating a meal is *"sihk fahn"*—which translates to "eat rice." (I can hear the reader now: "Is he *sure* this isn't the 'Xenophobia' essay?" It isn't. And we're getting to xanthan gum, I promise.)

However rice-focused the Chinese diet, it's got nothing on the corn-centrism of the North American one. In Chinese food, rice, at least, has the decency to appear under its own name. Corn, however, is like a Cold War spy—receiving limitless financial support from the U.S. government and using an endless, disorienting string of pseudonyms and *noms de guerre,* making it almost impossible to keep track of. There are the obvious—cornstarch, corn syrup and cornmeal—and the relatively easy to spot for the semi-informed, like glucose and fructose. But the website LiveCornFree.com (a slogan that to my mind would've made for an even better New Hampshire licence plate) lists more than fifty euphemisms for the stuff, from ascorbic acid to zein, and some of them are positively hieroglyphic: decyl glucoside, ferrous gluconate, magnesium stearate and, you guessed it: xanthan gum, that ooey, gooey, viscous treat.

Xanthan gum apologists will tell you that the fermentation process leaves no corn protein and that the gum is, therefore, safe for the allergic, but I have my suspicions. It also seems, on principle, to be worth calling out corn's anodyne-sounding aliases (in fact "anodyne" itself sounds like it could be something made from corn). Having a corn allergy means reading ingredients lists with the painstaking attention of a lawyer. And you'll be just as popular as lawyers are when you inform your kind dinner party hosts that "No," after having spent the last three minutes reading the side of the tub, you "won't be able to have any ice cream, because it's got xanthan gum."

When he first informed me of my allergies, the doctor said, if I wanted, I could eliminate any or all of the foods from my diet just to see how it felt; I could then reintroduce them and see how that went. It was my sincerest, deepest hope that the screenwriters and populists were right—that food allergies were bourgie bullshit, that the whole thing was just a cultural placebo effect (incidentally, with my corn allergy, I couldn't comfortably take placebos—most pills use cornstarch as a binding agent).

Sadly, I discovered they are legitimate. Almost right after my post-allergic purge, I lost most of the chronic light-headedness, dizziness and vertigo that I'd been suffering from (the rest I chalk up to anxiety); I stopped my semi-regular schedule of throwing up, something I'd always attributed to a very sensitive gag reflex that would forever keep me out of the fields of pornography and marketing. I thought back with shame on all the sushi restaurants I had slandered as unhygienic, simply because I'd found their dynamite rolls more explosive than intended. And any hope that it was all psychosomatic was quashed any time I would *unknowingly* consume rice or corn; a family friend who happens to be a prominent Toronto physician was ready to send me for a scan to see if my brain was bleeding after I'd complained of inexplicable dizziness and vomiting during a trip to the city. Before the test, though, we discovered that my mother-in-law's "whole wheat" English muffins, which I'd been eating every morning of our visit for breakfast, were made of cornmeal.

Chances are high that corn is lurking somewhere in any remotely processed foodstuff, usually obscured by a false identity. That's what corn does, see? It insinuates itself into every corner of our society and our way of life, using its inscrutability and deceptiveness to catch us off guard—okay, at this point I, too, am unclear whether this is the "Xenophobia" essay.

I chose xanthan gum as a metonymic stand-in for the real issue: in late-capitalist food culture, corn wears many disguises, xanthan gum among them, and we oughtn't trust any foodstuff that won't straightforwardly present itself as being whatever it is. To paraphrase Shelley's "The Mask of Anarchy":

> And many more Destructions played
> In this corny masquerade,
> All disguised, even to the eyes,
> As cellulose, maltitol, starch in pies.

Y FOR YUPPIES

for Yuppies

WHEN MY WIFE was pregnant with our daughter, a group of our very kind and generous friends told us that they were all chipping in to buy us a stroller as a baby shower gift; the implication was that we should go nuts, choosing one of those top-of-the-line jobs that look like a stylized cluster of speech balloons from an Ikea-themed comic book—strollers in which you can be almost guaranteed to find a baby wearing an amber teething necklace, strollers pushed by fathers who have an affected interest in soccer.

Since I had been reading books about how to be a dad (an already suspiciously bourgeois course of study, cemented by our later decision to take a prenatal class and breastfeeding clinic: "So, you're saying the milk comes out of the *mother's* breast?"), the task of choosing the stroller came down to me. The decision would come to disappoint nearly everyone involved but the baby and me. My father and I went down to the department store and I tested all of the floor models for the many practical qualities indicated as important in the book I was reading: could they be easily steered, with one or both hands; were they simple to fold; et cetera. To this list, though, I added my own questions: How much space in a café would this stroller take up? Will this stroller make us look like rich dickheads? Can we eschew the tasteful royal blues and rusty reds of contemporary affluent carriages for the ugly greys of the strollers of my own childhood? This reverse snobbery played a leading role in my choosing a boxy, relatively down-market, fog-coloured stroller whose selection was anticlimactic not only for my wife but for the friends who were paying for it; it was like they'd offered us a trip to any city in the world and we'd chosen Hamilton, Ontario. One of the guys who was initially supposed to chip in was dropped from the roster of gift-givers because his contribution was no longer necessary. The stroller was safe (so okay, Hamilton's not a precise analogy), practical and ugly, which made it perfect for me. As a cultural signifier, it suggested struggling and unpretentious new parents, as opposed to being a rolling, luxury holding tank for the arcanely named and blissfully unvaccinated Ivy Leaguers of tomorrow.

In the 1987 film *Baby Boom*, Diane Keaton plays a quintessential mid-'80s big-city yuppie, whose lifestyle is upended when she becomes legal guardian to a toddler. It says a lot about how much things have changed, culturally, that baby-and-yuppie was once seen as the sort of comic incongruity that could carry a movie, like cop-with-a-dog-for-a-partner or Arnold Schwarzenegger-teaches-kindergarten. Over the course of the film, Keaton's character realizes that she can be both a parent *and* a yuppie by selling high-end natural baby foods, and in this sense the picture was nothing short of prophetic: not only is parenthood now seen as compatible with yuppiedom, it is its nirvana—an endless opportunity for conspicuous consumption and otherwise competitive purchases, without the guilt of self-indulgence. Child-rearing has also, for some, removed the last moral or shame-based obstacles to acquiring the salient political features of yuppiness. Folks who would never dream of buying an organic mattress or lending support to the neighbourhood watch surveillance that accompanies any pioneering wave of gentrification find they can easily project these decisions onto the wee ones in their care and "do it for the baby." The result is that today, no handsome semi-detached duplex is complete without a jogging stroller on the front porch.

I could flatter myself by insisting that my stroller-purchase anti-elitism was a function of the cultural distance between yuppies and me, but really it was a fetishistic disavowal of how close we are. Cara and I may not have done a doula-assisted home birth into a kiddie pool filled with almond milk, but there are plenty of other cultural markers of our encroaching onto yuppie territory. The most telling, probably, is that I was thirty-three when my daughter was born, making me the first man in my patrilineal line not to become a father at precisely age twenty-five in one hundred years (perhaps not coincidentally, I was also the first Demers raised Anglican instead of Catholic). Now, thirty-three over twenty-five may not seem like an enormous difference, but it's worth remembering that it *is* when (a) like me, you have a persistent, usually subliminal but occasionally explicit belief that, like your mother, and her father, you won't make it to forty and (b) you consider the social mobility that can occur in those years, particularly if you don't already have a child. The year I turned twenty-eight—the same age my dad was when he became a father for the second time—I made just enough to hurdle the poverty line by a few thousand dollars (in most of the years leading up to that, I hadn't been so lucky). In those twelve months, I had worked as a groundskeeper, a crossing guard and in a tea shop. The following year, I was hired to be on a TV show, published two books and performed at the Just for Laughs comedy festival, and made around quadruple the salary of the previous year. Admittedly, the year after *that,* the show was cancelled and I made just over half of that, a healthy chunk of which was severance—but it was still more than double what I'd made during my final year in the proletariat. The die was now cast and I was quasi-firmly ensconced in the much-vaunted creative class, making me one of the eponymous young urban professionals of yuppiedom.

There were other signs, too: both my wife and I had university degrees when our daughter was born (a graduate degree, in my wife's case), which neither of my parents had when I'd come along. We were older, better educated, better paid; we drank stevia-sweetened soft drinks (*Breaking Bad*'s stevia-swilling yuppie villain, Lydia, would come to cement this particular trope in the popular imagination), drove a Toyota of which we were the very first owners and our child was half-European, half-Asian, which in Vancouver is the only ethno-cultural category whiter than white. Some are born yuppies, but we were having it thrust upon us.

The two urban categories held in greatest contempt are the yuppies and the hipsters. Both terms are used vaguely and sometimes contradictorily, and sometimes the two are even used interchangeably, which I think is a sort of imprecision bordering on unforgivable. As I see it, generally, hipsters are younger and employed beneath the level of their education and are, therefore, in possession of a surfeit of time, allowing them to develop increasingly intricate and sophisticated tastes; yuppies, being more established in their careers, have less time but more money, driving them towards acquisitions (cultural, architectural, vehicular, sartorial, nutritional) that are more abundant but also more prepackaged and pedestrian. This is why yuppies and hipsters can't possibly be the same thing—if you are young, live in the city and have some money, one of the only ways to avoid being labelled a yuppie is to be hip (the other is to have an ugly socialist realist stroller). The paradox is that although the two groups are technically hated, hipsters do have great taste and yuppies do have lots of somewhat blandly wonderful stuff. So whereas most of us would do whatever we could not to be *reduced* to either of these two categories, a large part of us does want to be in them.

The fear of becoming, or being seen as becoming, a yuppie is an understandable one but silly, and any energy spent kicking against it could better be spent in a spin class. Tomorrow, climate change could melt the bottom out from underneath semi-

post-industrial late capitalism. Or the ongoing political and economic project to eliminate the chubby, sunburned middle class
entirely could finally succeed. In either scenario, my family's
precarious ersatz affluence would disappear, in which case I'd
have bigger things to worry about than my cultural authenticity.
Furthermore, as my thirties crest, the remaining space in which I
have to be called or to think of myself as "young" (the state of being
that puts the *y* in yuppie) shrinks rapidly, like arugula wilting in a
hot pan. In the meantime, as I become incrementally more finan-
cially stable, and precipitously more exhausted and therefore be-
reft of the vast pools of energy that it takes to remain interesting,
then, well, the handwriting is on the exposed brick wall. If the ingredients are there—if you're a well-educated city dweller with a
decent career and non-catastrophic prospects—fighting becoming a yuppie is like trying to stay awake against a Xanax or a Klon-
opin you've just taken during a late-night movie: it will be warmer,
a little boring, but much more comfortable when you just give in.

for Zzz

JUST BEFORE I SAT down to type this final essay, a new con-
troversy came across the indignation-delivery service of social media: Scandinavian art-throb Karl Ove Knausgaard—the
Norwegian author who wrote his wide-ranging encyclopedic
memories into a bestselling multi-volume series with the slightly queasy-making title of *Min Kamp* (which means "my struggle,"
just like the other guy's book)—visited Newfoundland, where he
observed, with great disgust, the unseemly fatness of the locals.

Could anything be more boring than this? Yet another lithe,
sophisticated European commenting, as if for the first time,
upon North American obesity; since the time of Columbus,
there seems to have been no European on earth who could resist
the desire to cross the Atlantic and claim to discover what everybody already knew (all the way back in 2006, Garrison Keillor
was yawning over the "Freaks, Fatties, Fanatics & Faux Culture
Excursion beloved of European journalists"). Could anything be
more boring than me, a fat North American, taking offence at
Knausgaard's deep navel-gazing and tweeting my umbrage? Yet
that's precisely what happened. And next week, it will be something else. This is the style of our contemporary social discourse.
Adolph Reed, Jr., an American political scholar who is handsome

enough to put forward the kind of invincible pessimism that we're otherwise loathe to let people get away with, compares this sort of argument to kayfabe, "a term of art in pro wrestling." It is, he explains, "a participating audience coming together around what everyone knows on some level is the fictional quality of the sport, but coming together around a shared commitment to treat it as though it were real."

About a year and a half ago, in 2013, as President Barack Obama was considering going to war with Bashar al-Assad of Syria, I found myself struck with a kind of political vertigo. As I was airing my (anti-intervention) opinions into the digital ether, I realized I was having the same conversation—with the same allies and same opponents—as I had had two years earlier, about Libya. Not a similar conversation, mind you, but exactly the same one, with nearly everyone lined up in exactly the same place. Every time a possible war rolls along, at least a handful of leftists will make a break for respectability by supporting it, and a couple of craggy old military types will have a Jesus-not-this-shit-again epiphany that leads to them criticizing it, but otherwise, the teams are remarkably static. It suddenly struck me that we would probably be having these Sisyphean non-debates for the rest of my life—one TV pundit rolling a green-screen rock up a green-screen hill, his opposite number rolling it back down.

People are fond of observing that life is short; it's a phrase they repeat enough to make one question how much they really believe it. Life, in fact (although it's exceedingly obvious to point this out) is the longest thing that any person has ever experienced. It seems even longer because it's undramatic—which is different from saying that it's uneventful. Dramatic things happen in every human life, but it's rare that they move the story, or any story, forward in a meaningful way. Drama is narrative, a causal link of events that come together to our satisfaction. This is emphatically not what life is like. In an early episode of *The Sopranos*, Christopher Moltisanti—whose story is exemplarily human, consisting of alternations between depression, the elusive search for meaning in community, retreat into sensual pleasure and addictive escape and, finally (spoiler), death at the side of a highway—tells his boss: "I don't know, Tony. It's like just the fuckin' regularness of life is too fuckin' hard for me or something. I don't know." Earlier on, he explains to another mobster how characters in film are supposed to make a journey, to have an arc—"Where's my arc?" he asks plaintively. Christopher is panicked that his life doesn't have a narrative structure; it's too bad he didn't have Knausgaard's agent (I kid!).

If we struggle, like Karl or Christopher, to find an arc in our individual lives—if Douglas Coupland is correct in observing that as the twenty-first century unfolds, "it will become harder to view your life as 'a story'"—we've almost completely jettisoned the idea that we have one as a species. The term "grand narrative" is never used as anything but a pejorative; on campus, it's as politically acceptable as the term "Grand Dragon." If nobody believes anymore that, for instance, we're moving along in a difficult but discernible journey through slavery, feudalism and capitalism on the way to socialism, then our shared history becomes as loose, undefined and uninspiring as a Newfoundland waistline. In this scenario, history becomes not only violent, bloody, exploitative and self-defeating but *boring*.

The advice given in circumstances like these—both individual and historical—is often to become more grounded in the present moment. Before writing this, I took a walk around the lake by my house and there was a bald eagle in a tree surrounded by crows, and even if my life is absurd and pointless in a cosmic sense, it's nice to see birds. I saw a robin, which always makes me feel closer to my mother, whose name that was. I told the bird, "I'm almost done," referring to the book, and although in a few months or years the satisfaction and crisp definition of this moment may soften and sink back down into the longer non-story of my life, at the moment, it feels good. I have ordered the sprawling nightmares of my world onto a grid that is artificial but socially recognizable: the alphabet. It's not narrative, but it's a shape.

Present-mindedness in our historical and political lives is slightly more treacherous territory—the non-utopian focus on the present, on the world as it is right now, has called forth an army of smug assholes under the banner of pragmatism (although I imagine the first thing a bunch of pragmatists would do would be to ditch the banner—*Where's the utility? It's just another thing to carry, bro!*). Living for today is easiest for centrists, conservatives pine for yesterday and the whole point of leftism is tomorrow. In 2012, the art historian and left-winger T.J. Clark made a passionately downcast appeal in the journal *New Left Review* "for a left with no future," asking us to imagine what it might look like to be an anti-capitalist who never thought the good guys were going to win but continued to intervene politically anyway. His piece called for politics "in a tragic key."

There's no piece of writing that I can think of—that I've read in the past, say, ten years—that has stuck with me more than Clark's. I can't remember the circumstances of the first time I read it, but the second time was in the suite of a resort on the very edge of the Pacific Ocean, during what was supposed to be a romantic trip before my wife and I shared the news of her pregnancy with everyone we knew. Instead, the trip took on a depressive aspect, in the shadow of an election that hadn't gone our way. A leftist politician whom I greatly admired, and continue to admire, and who had been all but guaranteed to become premier of British Columbia—one paper had run the headline "If This Man Kicked a Dog, He'd Still Win the Election"—was routed. I was hit hard by the loss, especially because, over the course of the campaign, I had been secretly working for him as a ghostwriter—writing jokes.

My jokes didn't save us. Nevertheless, I'm still not sure I'm ready for the tragic key. As I hope is clear to the reader by now, in matters both personal and political, intimate and historic, my preferred key is tragicomic. It's much truer to life, I think, and to history. It's less boring. And it's much more fun.

Acknowledgements

THERE ARE TWO people especially without whom this book would not exist; I'll start with one and end with the other. Trena White not only encouraged me to write another book but understood exactly what this one was about from the moment I pitched it to her. Through the vicissitudes of a great publisher's bankruptcy, limbo, then rebirth, Trena's role with the book evolved and changed, but she has consistently been a shepherd to it, and I couldn't be more grateful to have her as an editor.

I offer deep, genuine thanks to everyone at Douglas & McIntyre for their unflappable patience (at least I never noticed it flapping as I tried and failed to write a book on time during a dramatic year of birth and also illness in our family). Thank you to my excellent agent, John Pearce, and to Caroline Skelton for the title. Thank you also to D&M's amazing team, including Anna Comfort O'Keeffe, Corina Eberle, Brianna Cerkiewicz, Zoe Grams, Shirarose Wilesky and Carleton Wilson. Thank you, Eduardorama, for the incredible illustrations.

Thank you to my father, Daniel; my brother, Nicholas; and everyone else in my family for your love and encouragement. Thank you to Catherine and David O'Keefe for so often offering a place to write. Thank you to my colleagues and students at UBC Creative Writing, particularly my pal Steven Galloway. Thanks to Derrick O'Keefe and Tejpal Swatch for their feedback on early portions of the manuscript, and to Marcus Youssef, who kicked around ideas with me on "Adolescence," "Capitalism," "Tax Rage," "Valet Parking" and "Union-Busting" for another project, which helped shape the way they showed up here. Thank you to Mark Leier for pointing out the similarities between Metropolises. Anyone who has read Toby Rollo's Twitter feed will see my debt to him in thinking through white anti-racism as it relates to anti-colonialism in the essay on settlerism; I'm also indebted to some of Hayden King's terrific and important writing on land and sovereignty. Several of the pieces included here grew out of jokes, essays and rants that appeared elsewhere, including on CBC Radio's *The Debaters* and *Definitely Not the Opera*. Thank you to the CBC, the taxpayers who pay for it and everybody who doesn't vote for the guys who are trying to kill it. Thanks to Richard Side, Kevin Chong, Pat Kelly, Erik Rutherford, Deb Williams, Nicholas Perrin and Am Johal for providing the initial impetus and/or home for some of the prototypes for these essays.

To my daughter, Joséphine: it would be odd to thank you, since not only were you of absolutely no help in writing this book, but—since most of the writing coincided with the first sixteen months of your life—you were pretty much the main impediment to it. If you're reading this, I want you to know: you were totes worth it. (Do kids still say "totes" in the future? Anyway: I love you more than anything.)

Finally, the other person without whom there would absolutely not be a book: my brilliant, loving and beloved wife, Cara Ng. I still believe you sorta got a bum deal when they were handing out husbands, but I don't ever for a second forget how lucky I am to have you. Thank you for this.